Early Childhood Media Mastery:

A Complete Guide to Teaching Smart and Responsible Media Use

Michelle Ellisor, LMFT

The information in this volume is not intended as a substitute for consultation with healthcare professionals. Individual health concerns should be evaluated by a qualified professional.

Library of Congress Cataloging-in-Publication Data

Ellisor, Michelle
        Early Childhood Media Mastery : A Complete Guide to Teaching Smart & Responsible Media Use

ISBN: 978-1534741553

Library of Congress Control Number: 2016917128
CreateSpace Independent Publishing Platform, North Charleston, SC

*To my daughter, Ty, Dawn, Rozi, Dan
and my own wonderful parents-
thank you for your love, help, support, and
inspiration*

Contents

Introduction

What is early childhood media mastery? Media mastery is the ability to fully understand digital media well enough to use it responsibly and with creativity. It is a group of skills that your child can develop over time. Media mastery will enable your child to use technology to solve problems. This is very different than simply developing a proficiency with basic media use, which involves only understanding the basics of how to use a given product or device. Technology will continue to evolve quickly during our lifetime, and developing media mastery will be a key component of navigating our world with success. There are significant advantages and some risks to media use at different ages and stages in your child's life. This book will set out specific early childhood guidelines to help you understand how media fits into your child's development. Children who learn to utilize media in ways that are healthy, and that contribute to their problem solving ability, will have a significant advantage in our technology-driven world.

In the last few decades, digital media has changed dramatically. The impact on our day-to-day lives is undeniable. Digital devices have evolved from tools and games used for work or entertainment into omnipresent personal devices. These devices connect us to family, friends, work, social networks, and endless data, both personal and public, which are all woven seamlessly into our daily functioning. Twenty years ago, the biggest media questions for parents of young children were related to television viewing and to the growing number of video game platforms, most of which targeted school-aged children and older. Fast-forward to today, and technology is being marketed to our children practically from *birth*. With the advent of small touchscreen devices, even babies can technically engage with some very advanced technology.

The most significant change, especially where children are concerned, is the move to *integrated* use. Our technology is now with us all the time, and it significantly impacts our lifestyle and day-to-day functioning. An important process happens in the brief moment before we turn on or turn off a device, and that is the choice we make to engage or disengage with technology. In today's world, a lot of technology never gets turned on or turned off, so we don't always make that choice. In fact, it often actively solicits our attention with beeps and other notifications, instead of the other way around. For adults, this kind of integrated use can have numerous benefits. When appropriately mediated, it can often add meaningful connections to people and to important information, which can improve our quality of life. Children, on the other hand, especially young children, are not ready for this level of sophisticated use. They have a lot of learning to do before they become media masters. This book aims to help break down the steps and stages to accomplish this learning process, so that parents can begin to successfully guide children from their earliest years.

Digital media is no longer a parenting issue which can be addressed in adolescence or when children begin school. The continued movement towards integrated technology use, which is predicted to become even more ingrained in our day-to-day lives, requires parents to address some complex issues early on. The way that most adults use digital media might feel simple and straightforward because it is designed to assist people in a seamless fashion. The reality though, is very different. Consider for a moment, watching your child learn to stand up and take a few steps. This is a good reminder of all the balance, coordination and strength it takes to walk. It is something that once learned, we take for granted. Likewise, we are not aware of all the skills that we use as we engage with technology.

I grew up using maps and verbal or written directions to find places, and because of that I possess some basic navigation skills which are still important in this day and age, especially if, *God forbid*, my cell phone ran out of battery power. Aside from finding a nearby gas station or getting myself home, my navigation skills are also related to important concepts of spatial awareness that help me understand where I am in the world. If you really consider the knowledge and skill set of a two-year-old, it becomes clear that there is a lot that our children need to learn before they can really understand and therefore appropriately utilize technology. They are not ready to take these tools for granted. My daughter will need to learn about the sun, clouds, rain, and the seasons before she begins using my weather app to decide what to wear today. In fact, she will need to learn how to dress herself and about weather-appropriate clothing. Later on, as a media master, she may be able to utilize real-world data and technology to create a road traffic weather warning system for her high school science project. Until then, she does not need to be taught to use a touch screen and she will probably figure out pull-down menus much more quickly than I did, but she does have a lot of much more complex real-world ideas and concepts to master before she can take on this project.

There are also important safety concerns related to early childhood use of advanced technology, especially exposure to passive screen media. When media is introduced inappropriately or is overused in childhood, there can be significant developmental concerns related to your child's health and wellbeing. There is research-based evidence that misuse can cause long-term problems. These issues will be addressed in chapter two. This information has also been incorporated into all guidelines and suggestions presented in this book. Technology will indeed become an important part of our children's lives, both now and in the future, especially as they become adults. The goal of this book is to help parents learn to introduce digital media intentionally, and with appropriate caution. Technology can certainly provide many benefits for our children. Current research which demonstrates how digital media can enhance learning is highlighted throughout the book whenever relevant. The most important thing to remember is that children need to be *taught* to use digital media. They need to learn about *what* they are doing, and they need to learn skills for appropriately managing their use, so they are not harmed by misuse or overuse.

Many parents don't feel like *media masters* themselves, but you don't have to be a technology expert to teach your children how to understand and use digital media in a healthy way. Part one of this book will introduce general guidelines related to different aspects of media use,

including use of different kinds of devices, forms of media
and important skills for responsible media use. Part two
will break these concepts down into age-specific chapters
which will include age-specific suggestions and additional
information for each age group. Part three will introduce
information related to individualizing these guidelines and
recommendations for your own unique family. Part four
provides charts and forms which break down concepts
from the book into easy to use (and easy to remember)
tools. These charts and forms can be copied or printed for
your personal use. They may be helpful as quick sheet
reminders of important concepts or to create your
individual family media use guidelines. My hope is that in
reading this book, you will gain the knowledge, skills and
confidence to guide your child towards media mastery.
You may even end up becoming more of a media master
yourself!

Michelle Ellisor, LMFT

PART I: MEDIA MASTERY GUIDELINES

Ch. 1
A Developmental Approach

"Any fool can know. The point is to understand."
-Albert Einstein

You wait and watch excitedly as your child takes her first steps. You cherish the moment when you first hear "dadda" and you cheer the first time she poops in the toilet. These are early developmental milestones that most parents watch. Your child will accomplish many more milestones along the way, each at her own pace. You may hear your child's Pre-K teacher talk about how many words she should have in her vocabulary before she begins Kindergarten. Her P.E. teacher might also comment on her strength and ability to throw and catch a ball. Both teachers may discuss her ability to follow instructions and share with other children. These are all developmental milestones that can help indicate that your child is learning. Human development is unique in that each child will usually learn the same things within a similar time frame, but will do it their own way and at their own pace. Each child becomes a human adult, but they all learn to become their own unique person. Technology can be great when it helps individualize learning. Likewise, the way that children learn about technology also needs to be tailored to their development.

Creating new media guidelines for your child requires a balance of understanding the stages of child development and understanding your child's individual needs. Think about the way that you first learned about written language. We all learn the alphabet much the same way: we repeat the ABC song and practice writing each letter on jumbo three-lined paper. We each master the different letters and skills individually and at our own pace, until one way or another they come together for us and we master the tools that we need to write. This is the *child development* aspect of the process. Most children will master these skills within the same general time frame. The same tools can be used to help most children accomplish this task with some individualized assistance. Still, if you and I were both to handwrite this sentence, while both sentences could presumably be read and understood, they would look totally different. We would also probably dot our i's and cross our t's in our own way while writing. We are all a little bit unique in our process. I might have struggled to memorize letters but have had an easier time mastering handwriting. You might have learned your letters quickly but struggled to learn to create legible letters. This is the *individual strengths and needs* aspect of the process. To effectively teach both of us, our teacher needed a solid understanding of typical child development and to recognize our individual challenges. Similarly, as a parent, you will need to recognize the specific skills that your child is working on in order to introduce new media at times and in ways that promote her learning.

This book uses a developmental approach to creating media guidelines for children. This approach takes into account a child's natural progression of growth in areas of cognitive (thinking), physical, social and emotional development. This is essential, as children are not born with all of the skills and abilities necessary to use and make good choices about media. There is a natural progression of maturity, which will allow your child to gradually learn new things and understand more and more complex ideas. This progression is used to determine important developmental milestones in early childhood and throughout your child's development. Even though each child develops skills and abilities at his or her own pace, generalized guidelines can help make certain that your child has an optimal learning experience. The approach taken in this workbook incorporates an understanding of the development of the skills and abilities required to gradually master the use of technology. It also leverages research about how inappropriate use of technology may actually hinder development. The result is the creation of a set of usable guidelines, meant to be applied in conjunction with your unique understanding and knowledge of your child.

An important concept throughout this book is the focus of developing mastery versus basic proficiency. New technology and media use is increasingly becoming an essential part of people's social and work lives. Even outside of the technology sector, knowledge and understanding of new media use is considered an important asset in the workplace. Employees, employers and entrepreneurs alike have a significant advantage if they are able to use technology to increase efficiency and improve communication. The ability to apply critical thinking skills to the use of technology in the workplace will continue to become more and more important, and it will require some level of media mastery. This does not mean that your child has to develop an intricate understanding of how computers work or that she will need to be able to program or create new technology to be successful. The type of mastery described in this workbook refers to the ability to use and understand new media well enough to use it responsibly and creatively to solve problems.

Here's an example of what this kind of mastery looks like in the workplace. A busy accountant is interested in using technology to help her save time while still providing good customer service during tax season. She decides that a new program could help her by automatically sending reminder emails with instructions to customers who have not yet turned in their paperwork for tax preparation. The program would be customized to the manner in which paperwork is received, possibly by fax, email or by delivery to the office. She decides that this program will check in the appropriate documents and confirm that all paperwork has been received. This will allow it to send personalized emails with reminders to those who have not yet turned in their paperwork or a confirmation if they have. This program could save her an immense amount of time and energy during her busiest time of year by helping her keep paperwork organized and assisting her with communication to customers. She would likely call on other experts to create this project, but the accountant needs a level of media mastery in order to visualize the basic idea and understand what might be possible.

It is impossible to completely know what kinds of creative uses of technology and new media will be unveiled in the future because the field advances so rapidly. The only way to help your children be prepared is to help them develop a broad level of mastery and knowledge. It is also very important to keep in mind that for very young children, traditional early childhood goals related to their physical, cognitive (thinking), social and emotional development are paramount, and should always take precedence over learning any specific knowledge or skill. In her earliest years, your child's mind acts like a sponge, absorbing an immense amount of information about her world. She is wired to learn just by being in and exploring the world around her, not by being taught a specific skill. This is why babies learn to talk simply by being exposed to language and to the communication of others. Attempting to teach very young children using traditional strategies that are created for older children is unnecessary, and may even distract from the type of exploratory learning your child is meant to do.

Remember that there will be plenty of time for your child to learn about new media and technology. Computers and tablets are more commonly being introduced in school, and eventually a variety of devices will become a regular part of her academic and social life.

It is therefore even more important that other time-sensitive types of learning occur in early childhood. In childhood there are "windows of opportunity", during which children are best able to develop important skills and abilities that they need for continue learning. If inappropriate media use or other negative experiences interfere with development during these early windows of opportunity, your child might experience significant challenges throughout childhood and even into adulthood. Media use guidelines can help you avoid some of these potential pitfalls. They can also help you to use new media in ways that take full advantage of these windows of opportunity and that actually promote learning.

Areas of Child Development

Cognitive Development-
Includes the construction of thought processes, memory, problem solving and decision making
Physical Development
Refers to physical growth and the development of large and fine motor skills, which allow a child to use their bodies and develop physical skills
Social Development
Includes the development of social skills for communicating with others and for developing relationships
Emotional Development
Refers to a child's ability recognize, express, understand, and regulate his or her emotions

---

The Media Mastery Approach

Early Childhood Media Mastery: A Complete Guide to Teaching
Smart & Responsible Media Use

The media mastery approach in this book is based on the understanding that children need a frame of reference in order to truly learn about technology. If they do not have an understanding of significant background information, they may hit a wall when it comes to more advanced concepts or uses of technology. Teachers know that their students learn more effectively when they already have some basic knowledge of a concept area. This is why a general overview of basic concepts and facts are often taught first and more detailed lessons are then later used to expand on this information. For instance, a child needs to have a solid understanding of numbers and counting before he or she is able to learn addition. Unfortunately, some children do learn to do math by rote memorization of lessons without fully grasping the basic concepts that make these problems solvable. These children then struggle immensely as their math lessons get more and more complicated. This is also why a child who can pick up a device and immediately start *"using it"* is not necessarily completely tech-savvy.

Real learning, at any age, involves assimilating new information within the framework of systems and concepts that we already understand. A technology equivalent to this concept is an adult who understands that Wikipedia is an open-source online encyclopedia, created through the collaborative effort of a community of users, which contains articles that change and may or may not be accurate depending on the reliability of the contributors. A child or teenager was never introduced to the old concept of an encyclopedia, and does not have knowledge about what makes a source reliable or acceptable in an academic setting, may have difficulty learning how to appropriately utilize this resource for school. (Actually, there are many adults right now who don't have a full understanding of what a wiki is or how Wikipedia works.) The teenager who does possesses this knowledge along with appropriate background knowledge about encyclopedias and academic sources is at a significant advantage because he or she is able to utilize this resource fully and appropriately.

This book outlines an appropriate progression for the introduction of technology and new media to children in a manner that allows them to utilize both their newly developing abilities and prior knowledge when learning about technology. Children must first begin to learn about their physical world and about very basic concepts of physics, communication, language and life before they begin learning about and with technology. The media mastery method allows you to take advantage of the way that your child naturally grows and learns in early childhood. It allows for an important translation process to occur, so that your child can learn about the tools that he or she is using and truly master their use.

From Baby to Toddler

Between birth and age three, your child is very affected by her surroundings, and her learning environment is more important than ever. At this point her brain is equipped with more neurons or connections than it will ever have again. Her brain is going through a pruning process which allows her to create, strengthen and keep neural connections that will be relevant to her life. At this stage, your child's relationship with her primary caregivers is the most significant factor related to her healthy development. She needs to experience important environmental stimuli such as hearing words and language, touching, tasting and seeing a variety of objects and exploring her physical world. These things will significantly impact her future development, health, and learning ability. One of the most significant concerns about technology for babies and toddlers is it's potential to interfere with the amount and quality of time that they spend with caregivers and exploring the physical world. Technology can easily replace interactive time with a caregiver. It also creates a significant distraction which can impact a baby's ability to engage in normal play behavior.

Learning at this age is enhanced most by interaction with adult caregivers. Researchers, neuroscientists, and physicians now understand that humans evolved to be social and that our health and survival actually depend on interaction with others. A convergence of evidence shows that human connections shape our neural connections and influence how we mentally construct our reality. This process is critical during very early childhood development, but it actually continues to occur throughout life.[i] The most powerful and important learning experiences in early childhood involve interacting with caregivers. Any activity, whether it is play, looking at books, or making music becomes more beneficial to your child when you participate. There is no form of technology, device, or advanced robotics that can replace the human interaction that your child needs. Most new media devices are not recommended for children under the age of 3. As your child is introduced to new media, it will be important to consider how media can be used in conjunction with or even to encourage interaction with humans. For older children, new media can become a platform for indirect interaction with others, but it should never replace direct interaction.

Attachment Theory

Attachment theory in psychology refers to the emotional bond between a child and their primary caregiver(s), which is a primary means for early social and emotional development and which sets the stage for a child's future social relationships. The critical period for developing a secure attachment occurs in the first few years of a child's life, and a lack of success in this area has been linked to poor social and emotional adjustment and reduced intelligence. There is a growing amount of research which shows that young children can benefit more from direct engagement with an adult during any kind of learning activity or play. It seems that very young children are pre-programmed to learn by engaging with their caregivers.

Age Three and Beyond: Beginning Users

Around age three it becomes more appropriate to begin introducing new technology and media use to your child. This is when it will be important to really consider the translational processes necessary for your child to understand the tools that she is using. Your child will already be creating a framework for understanding how media fits into her world. New information can go unnoticed, be misunderstood, or ignored if it does not fit within your child's current understanding or frame of reference. A different type of learning process has to occur in order for your child to reframe her understanding so that she can make sense of this new information. She will need an understanding of real world experiences before she can understand and fully utilize technology as a tool. A beginner example is ebooks. If you have already spent time reading hard-bound books with your child, you may be able to present an ebook on a tablet or e-reader to your child. Clues such as a page-turn animation will help your child understand that the ebook is like the books they have already read. A PDF version of a book that can be read on a computer would obviously have less of these clues and would not be age appropriate. By the time your child is reading books in this format, she will have the background to understand that this is still a book. This is why young children should start by reading more traditional ebooks with their parents before they begin engaging with multimedia interactive ebooks.

This translation process may at first seem less important, but consider that most adults have learned to use technology at a time in their lives when they already possessed a full understanding of the world around them. Adults can easily grasp the connection of most forms of media to reality only because they are fully familiar with a non-digital world. Humans are not born with the ability to easily translate digital representations to reality; it is a learned process. When a child is introduced to digital reality at the same time that she is learning about the physical world, these concepts are not necessarily referenced appropriately. Children need to learn real-world concepts in order to understand technology better. It is important that children learn to see technology as a tool to enhance their lives, not as an equivalent experience. Otherwise they are more likely to develop unhealthy habits and an overdependence on technology.

Real-world learning is generally more effective for babies and toddlers. The *video deficit effect* was discovered during early research on infants, toddlers and television. This research shows that very young children learn better from a live demonstration than from video presentations.[ii] In one early study, toddlers were oriented to a room via two methods: in person and also through a video representation of the room. They were shown both to be sure that the toddlers could see that the video image was of the same live room. The children then watched via a television screen while an adult hid an object in the room. They were then allowed back into the room immediately afterwards to try to find the hidden toy. Only the children who were at least 2.5 years old were able to successfully find the toy, while two-year-olds were still unable to find it.[iii] We also know that processing information on a screen is a more cognitively demanding task, and young children require more time to process this kind of input than they do real-life input.[iv] Young children learn more quickly when a concept is presented by a real person. If video or screen representations are used to teach new concepts, young children will require more repetition before they grasp the concept. This is one of the reasons that the best way for young child to learn is to receive adult guidance or to collaborate with more capable peers, such as an older child or sibling.

In education, the power of mentoring and collaborative learning is explained with the concept of a *Zone of Proximal Development*. This zone describes the difference between what a student can accomplish or learn on her own and what that same student could achieve with direct guidance. It explains how a child can expand her learning and development when assisted by an adult or peer with a higher skill set. With guidance, a student is able to collaboratively problem solve with a teacher or peer to achieve learning previously beyond her individual ability. The collaborative process is essential because the student's teacher must provide just the right amount of assistance to allow a child to truly learn a concept, not just complete the task. This type of learning describes the process to achieve true mastery. Very young children require human mentoring to achieve this kind of mastery. This applies to your child's early development goals, his academic progress, and also to the goal of media mastery. When used appropriately, and when your child is ready, technology can help bridge this zone of proximal development at times by offering individualized learning opportunities for your child.

Lev Vygotsky's Zone of Proximal Development

Lev Vygotsky was a Russian psychologist who expanded on previous understandings of child development and who identified concepts which would lead to an entire Social Development Theory. This is significant because important aspects of his theory are being validated by current research in neurobiology.

A Note on The Importance of *the translation process* related to Media Mastery

This information is not meant to suggest that irreparable damage is done when children don't fully understand the technology that they are using. This is certainly not the case, and even when best efforts are made to introduce new media appropriately, some amount of initial confusion may occur. This is normal and expected. Problems arise when a child spends too much time being confused and has to relearn a lot of information about the world in order to catch up. It is likely that this child may fall behind in other aspects of her learning or miss out on lessons that she was unable to fully comprehend. If we consider the goal of media mastery, the hope is that your child will learn to use technology at an appropriate pace, in a way that will enhance her learning opportunities and allow her to excel at using these tools for the rest of her life.

Your Child's Unique Development

Each child follows their own unique development process, including growth and progress in different areas, at their own pace. There is not a specific developmental path and timeline that every child is meant to follow. Developmental guidelines are always meant to suggest a range of normal growth and development, so that you can tell if your child is generally ahead of or behind the normal curve. This allows parents to identify areas where their child may need more guidance or challenge. In this book, guidelines are used to make sure that new technology and concepts are introduced at ideal times, in order to promote your child's overall growth and development as well as her progress towards media mastery. It is important to also utilize your own knowledge of your child's unique personality and strengths to adjust these guidelines appropriately. You may also want or need to adjust your child's technology use and family guidelines to fit with your family culture and needs. Each family is different in terms of their access and overall usage of media and technology. If you are helping your child learn to use technology appropriately, and avoiding overuse, you should be able to avoid any potential harm.

There are certain situations which will require special consideration and may determine that your child needs media guidelines which differ from her peers or siblings. These include children who have been diagnosed with ADHD, Autism Spectrum Disorders, Anxiety or Depression, and children who may have experienced significant early trauma or have "at risk" factors such as poverty, family instability, or a community or environment with few resources, violence and discrimination. These situations will be discussed in more detail in Chapter 9.

Chapter Summary
- Human Interaction is the most important process during early childhood development.
- Direct/hands-on learning experiences can be gradually supplemented with media experience within a developmentally appropriate timeline.
- Media experiences should never be provided at the expense of interpersonal interaction and hands-on learning experience, and cannot replace either.

23

- Inappropriate media use in early childhood can cause harm to a child by replacing appropriate developmental opportunities.

Ch. 2
Do No Harm

"It is easier to build strong children than to repair broken men."
-Frederick Douglass

Every parent does their best to protect their child and prevent harm, but injuries and accidents are inevitable and part of life. While digital media offers exciting new educational and entertainment options, it also has the potential to impact children physically, mentally and emotionally. All family media guidelines should first aim to avoid harm. The goals are safety and media mastery, with safety being the first priority. In order to protect your children whenever possible, you need to know what to look out for. This chapter outlines the primary of areas of health and development which can be affected by misuse or overuse of technology. There are many other possibilities and theories related to negative effects which have been suggested, but this book includes only information which has been validated with credible research. It also highlights some of the areas that technology use has been shown to provide advantages.

There are numerous known correlations between technology use and long-term health and wellbeing. There is also evidence to suggest a direct causal link for certain negative impacts. You don't need to know all the technical differences between causal links and correlational research, but you should know that some research shows that certain things happen together, suggesting that they might be related somehow. Other research can actually show that one thing causes another to happen. This is significant because sometimes we learn that even though there is a correlation or connection between two things, one may not actually be causing the other. For instance, when analyzing data from the fire department someone might conclude that more fire damage occurs when more firefighters are sent to the scene of a fire because the amount of damage is correlated with the number of firefighters. Of course common sense tells us that more firefighters are sent to bigger fires, which are more likely to cause greater damage, so we are not likely to misinterpret this data. However, there are many instances where we cannot depend on our common sense to keep us from being misled, especially if we are studying something new. Often more research is needed to determine if a hypothesis is true, so recommendations can change over time. You will see that this is especially relevant to discussions about media violence. Still, sometimes the best thing we have to work with is a correlation. Even a loose connection can suggest a need for caution, especially if avoiding harm is the ultimate goal.

Research Term: Correlation	Research Term: Causation
When researchers find a correlation they are saying that that they found a relationship between two, or more, variables, such as study time and test scores. Correlations can be positive - so that as one variable (time spent studying) goes up, so does the other (test score); or they can be negative, which means that as one variable goes up (time spent playing video games) another goes down (grade point average). The trouble is that, unless they are properly controlled for, there could be other variables affecting this relationship that the researchers don't know about.	When researchers find causation it means that they were able to show that changes in one variable they measured directly caused changes in the other variable. This requires that participants are randomly assigned to an experimental group or a control group which does not experience the studied variable. If the experimental group shows change that is different than the control group, this allows scientists to prove that the outcome was caused by the studied variable. This kind of research requires more planning and control. In some cases it cannot be done for ethical reasons, because it is not acceptable to subject people to potential harm.

Children don't need digital media early in their life to become healthy, well-rounded adults. Wherever media use or misuse could jeopardize your child's health, it's important to remember that the knowledge of and skills for modern technology use can certainly be learned at a later date. There are no known developmental windows of opportunity for learning to use digital media and devices. In fact, there is some research to suggest that our brains adapt very quickly to incorporate these tools into the way we think, even in adulthood. A 2008 study on adults 55 years and older showed that after 5 days of internet use, the brains of digital newcomers (those with no internet surfing experience) had adapted to match the mental activity of their internet savvy counterparts. They were able to 'catch up', and their brains actually changed and adapted in a very short time.

That being said, it is not practical or necessary to avoid all digital media use. Technology is meant to be a tool we can use to improve our lives. After safety, our secondary goal involves finding ways to utilize media to benefit your family and your child. Developing media mastery will serve your child during his school years. It can help him avoid some typical teen pitfalls and assist him professionally and socially in his adult life. All Media Mastery guidelines seek to balance knowledge about potential benefits and potential harm from early childhood media use. Ultimately, you will still need to make decisions about what is most important to you as a parent and what will work best for your family. The following information is provided so that you can make more informed decisions based on the available research. Potential concerns related to your child's long-term physical health, sleep, cognitive development, academic success, mental health, and development of social skills are discussed. There are also significant short-term effects related to overuse or inappropriate use which are highlighted so that you can help your child avoid day-to-day challenges. An explanation and guidelines for age-appropriate media content, especially related to violence and advertising, are also included.

Long-Term Physical Health

Potential long-term health effects are one of the greatest concerns about childhood media use and they have been a significant focus of research efforts since the introduction and widespread use of home television sets. Most long-term studies have examined the effects of increased television viewing time, but more current research also examines video game, computer and internet use. There is currently very little quality research examining the use of tablets, smartphones and other newer devices because they are still new. For the time being it may be safest to assume that misuse or overuse of these devices could have some of the same negative effects as television, video games and computers. Most scientists theorize that traditional media use can have a negative impact on a child's health when it replaces other important activities and interaction, leads to increased sedentary time and/or exposes children to harmful advertising. Use of newer technology like smartphones and tablets can have the same consequences and therefore may have a similar negative impact. There is some evidence that interactive media use may avoid some of these problems, especially when games encourage activity, as in the Wii Sports or PlayStation Move games, but they may also bring with them new areas for concern.

Too much screen time, which is generally considered more than two hours per day, has been linked to a greater risk for obesity. In a recent study, teenagers who either increased or maintained a high level of TV time were at a much greater risk to become obese by early adulthood. Media use habits in childhood and parental media use habits are extremely influential in predicting a child's future media use. Obesity is more commonly occurring in childhood and, despite pediatric recommendations, young children are watching an excessive amount of TV and other screen media. Excessive TV time has been linked to high cholesterol in children. There is also some evidence that very young children who watch more than 2 hours of TV are more likely to develop asthma. Another huge concern is evidence suggesting that physical activity might not mediate the effects of excessive screen time. This means that even if your child exercises as much or more than recommended, he may still be at risk for long-term health effects if he spends too much time in front of a screen.

Advertising for low-nutritional quality food or junk food is also a significant problem. This is relevant to many forms of digital media use. TV commercials are notorious for targeting children in order to develop early brand preferences for fast-food. Advertisers are also taking advantage of new mediums which means that the internet and internet-based games are also potential sources of influence. Advergames, which are created by advertisers to exploit the powerful impact of modern gaming, can be especially insidious because even older users do not recognize their impact. They have also been cited as a way for advertisers to get around current restrictions on advertising to children. A review of numerous studies shows that children who are exposed to advertised food products have a strong preference for and request these foods. Almost all of the food advertised to children is high calorie and of low-nutritional value. These are the food choices that are most likely to lead to obesity and other health problems. Television viewing and video game play have also both been shown to increase a child's food consumption. When children regularly engage in sedentary behavior and then eat more calories than they have burned off, they are likely to gain weight which can eventually have serious long-term consequences.

Why does media time matter if my child is getting enough exercise?

Time spent with technology and especially screen media is usually sedentary time which involves sitting or lying down and very little energy expenditure. Excessive sedentary time is not healthy for humans, but it is especially concerning for children who are meant to spend most of their time moving and being active. Many people think about exercise when they consider healthy lifestyle choices, but they don't think about sedentary behaviors which are actually a separate concern. Getting in regular exercise sessions while also engaging in sedentary behavior most of the time is akin to exercising but not eating healthfully. Both choices affect your overall health and one good choice does not negate the need for addressing other areas.

Sleep

Getting the appropriate amount of quality sleep each night and developing good sleep hygiene early on is essential because it can impact your child's short-term and long-term functioning. Sleep deprivation actually has the potential to impact every aspect of a person's health. Typical sleep recommendations usually involve avoiding screens right before bedtime and keeping screens, especially TVs, out of children's bedrooms. The timing, quality and overall quantity of screen media use can impact your child's sleep.

Research has demonstrated a relationship between excessive screen time and poor sleep habits in children. Television and computer time have been linked to difficulty with sleep in childhood, especially as use exceeds recommended time limits. Increases in daily television time have also been demonstrated to result in increased sleep disruption. This certainly suggests a potential cause and effect relationship between more screen time and less sleep time. Viewing inappropriate media content including violent or frightening content can also cause sleep problems. A study involving a media use intervention program, which helped families to replace inappropriate media exposure with educational or prosocial content, showed that sleep problems could be improved with this type of media management. There is also some evidence that video-game play before bedtime could have an even greater effect on sleep than other media use. This could be due to the mental alertness required and/or the intense physiological arousal which can be a result of game play.

Cognitive Development

Play is essential to cognitive development in early childhood. Specifically, the type of play essential for development is imaginative free play and does not include video game play, organized activities, or sports. This imaginative 'pretend play' starts at a very young age. It is a primary method for children to explore and learn about the world around them and is also the foundation for their developing imagination. Imaginative play allows children to develop more complex cognitive processes, but it is dependent on time spent interacting with the physical world. Many professionals have expressed concern that entertainment media and digital games often replace traditional play for children, which could have serious consequences. Research does show that children who watch more TV engage in less pretend play and demonstrate less creativity and divergent thinking, which is essential for complex problem solving. Even educational or mentally stimulating games may present a concern if they are introduced at a young age, because they detract from imaginative play time and encourage more directed focus and play. These kinds of activities are more age-appropriate for older children. If they are introduced at a developmentally appropriate time they may provide some benefits, but given to children too early they could actually cause harm.

Academic Success

Children's media use habits can impact their learning and success at school. Screen time in early childhood may have a negative impact, but specific kinds of screen media use for older children can actually be beneficial. Watching TV before the age of 3 has been shown to predict lower academic achievement and test scores later on. Excessive TV time has been repeatedly shown to have a negative impact on academic performance at any age. Excessive screen time was originally considered more than 10 hours per week, and the more time children spend watching TV, the more it impacts their academic achievement. Children who have TV's in their room also underperform compared to their peers. *Low to moderate* TV viewing habits after age 3 have been linked to higher achievement and test scores. This positive association is greater when children watched primarily educational shows. Educational media use and parental co-viewing may increase potential learning opportunities for media use in children 3 and older. Parental co-viewing involves parents watching shows with their child, engaging with their child during screening, and discussing the content with them. An overview of research suggests that television viewing, especially in younger children, may have a negative impact on learning, particularly early reading, but that internet use can have a positive impact. In some cases, internet use has been linked to improved academic achievement and performance on standardized tests.

Based on the research, it is important to consider the content and function of screen time, especially TV viewing. If a child watches television for entertainment instead of engaging in potentially beneficial play, this may hurt academic achievement in the long run. On the other hand, a child might watch an educational program or practice reading on the internet instead of other entertainment. This kind of use might benefit them academically. When choosing educational media content, it is also important to note that not all educational media is equal. There is some evidence that educational media may be better suited for certain types of learning such as learning facts, but that it may be harder to use it to teach more complex concepts. Media use appears to help learners expand on their current understanding of a concept or to practice using it, but it may not be ideal for the initial learning process. This means that a child would need to be taught a new math lesson first, before they watch a show that drives home the same concepts. Educational media could enhance learning once the child understands the basic concepts but it does not necessarily offer an opportunity to replace the initial learning process. Once again research points to the importance of real world learning opportunities in early childhood. Media use should be viewed as a supplement.

Social Skills

This has been a major area of concern for teens communicating through digital devices and social media, but it's equally if not more important to consider the impact on younger children who are just learning social skills. There are two ways that media can impact a child's development of social skills. First, the content of the media that children view can depict or teach inappropriate or poor relationships and social skills. Secondly, the way that children use media and the way it's use is modeled can also impact social skills by replacing social interaction or interfering with face-to-face social interaction. Research shows that children who exceed screen time recommendations are more likely to have social problems. Children whose media use is monitored, so that they have less screen time and watch appropriate content, actually show more prosocial behavior and have better social outcomes. Remember that, as a parent, the behavior you model is especially important. There is growing concern about children having difficulty getting their parents attention because they are distracted by cell phones and other devices. When you frequently ignore your child or another person to attend to technology you teach your child to devalue interaction with those around them. This can also lead to increased acting out behaviors and poor social skills because your child may find that escalating behavior is the only way they get the attention they need from you.

Mental Health

Appropriate human interaction and connection is essential to developing and maintaining good mental health. Mental health can be impacted if technology interferes with the amount and quality of parent-child interaction and other social interaction which is required to develop healthy brain functioning and emotional skills. Television and computer use has been linked to indications of poor mental health in children, especially with excessive use. Early television viewing has also been associated with increases in acting out, aggressive behavior, emotional reactivity and less self-control. Inappropriate use or exposure through technology can also impact mental health, as is the case with cyberbullying and also with early exposure to pornography or other inappropriate content. Exposure to sexually explicit media content has been linked to emotional and psychological harm, increases in aggressive sexual behavior and to vulnerability to sexual abuse. Exposure to commercials and media advertising is also linked to poor self-esteem, body dissatisfaction and depression for some children and teens.

There are also special concerns for certain at-risk children including those with Attention Deficit Hyperactivity Disorder, anxiety or depression, early trauma experiences and traditional "at risk" factors. These children tend to interact with media and technology differently and may be more impacted by media content and use. This will be discussed further in Chapter 9.

Short-Term Effects of Screen Media Use or Overuse

- Significantly reduced verbal memory performance[v]
- Reduced emotional responsiveness[vi]
- Violent games increase violent thoughts and feelings[vii]
- Sensory overload[viii] and Increased Stress Response[ix] which can include the following symptoms:
    - Shutting down or avoiding others
    - Difficulty with focusing or concentration
    - Muscle tension
    - Restlessness
    - Fatigue

- o Difficulty sleeping
- o Anxiety
- o Headache
- o Upset Stomach

Violence and Media Content

A primary concern related to media content is often violent content and especially violent video games. There is evidence to suggest that violent content can be harmful to children or in some circumstance actually lead to more aggressive or violent behavior. It is worth noting that the total impact is sometimes exaggerated. Violent content is not the only thing parents need to be concerned about. Exposure to sexual content or alcohol, tobacco, and drug use in media can impact children and teens attitudes towards these topics and increase risk factors for early experimentation and use. In fact, all media content should be age-appropriate regardless of its theme or purpose. Even content without obvious topics of concern should be considered carefully because information and media messages can be misunderstood and cause confusion for children if they are not appropriately presented. There are many movies and shows that may at first glance appear to be kid-themed, such as many comic book based movies, but they are often not appropriate for children, especially young children. It's important to carefully review the content of all media to determine if it is appropriate for your child.

Risk of learning aggressive behavior from exposure to violent media increases when…

- the perpetrator is attractive
- the violence is seen as justified
- violence is seen as realistic, involving real-life weapons
- violence is rewarded, or at least not punished
- violence has little or no harmful consequences
- the violence is seen as funny

A combination of these factors becomes even more concerning.

Appropriate parental guidance early on can be a protective factor when it comes to media and gaming violence, because children with better emotional connections to adults and peers are at a lower risk. By limiting early media exposure, children can develop the social and emotional skills and connections that serve as protective factors.

Video Game Precautions

It's important to learn about any games your children are interested in playing. You cannot always rely solely on rating systems. The Entertainment Software Rating Board (ESRB) which issues ratings for games actually acknowledges some flaws in their own rating system, which is often focused on avoiding violence that is considered "graphic" or "explicit" but which may still contain elements that are known to increase the chances that a child will mimic violent behaviors. While long-term effects are more complicated, it is known that violent entertainment exposure can lead to a short-term increase in aggressive behavior in children and in adults. This is something to keep in mind when planning/scheduling entertainment time for your child, as a certain amount of downtime may be required to allow your child to regain full composure. Consider using additional sources for rating the age-appropriateness of games, such as *Common Sense Media* (www.commonsensemedia.org).

Media Content Guidelines		
CONTENT	AGE	EXPLANATION
Cartoon Violence/ Unrealistic Violence	4+	Until the age of 4 or 5 children will often have difficulty making judgements about whether or not something represented on a screen is potentially real or not. This ability will further develop by the age of 6 or 7, when a child will be more able to determine if depictions are reasonable or possible.
Unpunished Violence/ Violence without Consequences Content or characters that exhibit antisocial or discriminatory behavior or reinforce stereotypes,	7+	Until most children are about 7 yrs. old they will likely focus on whether a character was punished for engaging in violent behavior in order to determine if the behavior is right or wrong. Older children are able to consider the character's reason for engaging in violence and are less likely to see violent characters as role models even if they are

including gender stereotypes		attractive characters or their behavior goes unpunished. At seven you can begin talking to your child about discriminatory behavior and stereotypes. As part of media literacy discussions you can talk about the ways that media can reinforce these ideas. You should still try to avoid content that does not promote the positive values that fit with your family's belief system.
Violence as part of complex plots (ie. revenge, delayed consequences or outcomes)	9+	Children younger than 9 or 10 are often unable to make inferences about plot and subplot connections and may not make connections if there is a time-delay in a story or a break, such as a commercial.
Sexual Content that discusses and promotes healthy attitudes about sex and relevant consequences	11+	Curiosity, exploration and humor related to sexuality are a normal part of life for middle school children. Parents can utilize themes and scenes from movies and TV to help discuss this topic and address questions and real-world concerns.
Intricate Movie Plots Complex Video	13+	Preteens and Teens are developing metacognitive thinking skills which will allow them to understand and

Games with Violence Content with Alcohol, drug and tobacco use that demonstrates consequences of use		adjust their own thought processes related to the content they experience in entertainment.
Unmonitored exposure to entertainment violence and content with Alcohol, drug and tobacco use that does not demonstrate consequences of use or makes light of it	**17+**	All teens are subject to an adolescent egocentrism which means that while they may recognize a behavior as risky or dangerous, they are likely to underestimate their own personal risk due to feelings of invulnerability. There is some evidence that repeated exposure to entertainment violence in early adolescence can impair a teens ability to make good choices related to the use of weapons and physical aggression.[x]

Questions to Consider:

- How can you tell when your child has reached media overload?
- Do you struggle to set boundaries for avoiding your own misuse or overuse of digital media, including TV, gaming, social media and smart phone or internet use?

- What things do you do for yourself to make sure
  media is not impacting your health or
  relationships?

Michelle Ellisor, LMFT

Ch. 3
Hierarchy of Media Use

"Education is not the filling of a pail, but the lighting of a fire."
-William Butler Yeats

Your baby starts learning by touching, tasting, smelling and listening to the world around her. She will experience some of the most important growth and development in her brain in the first three years of her life. During this time her brain is especially sensitive to input from the environment around her and her earliest experiences will have some of the most profound effects on her future development and health. She will soon be ready to learn and explore even more. Between the ages of three and six the part of her brain related to attention will experience its greatest growth spurt. Then, around age seven she will change significantly again as the parts of her brain that control thinking and feeling grow rapidly. She will be especially prepared to learn through relationships and by interacting with other people and should be excited to learn about new topics. Innumerable changes occur in these early years in order to transform your child from a helpless infant into a capable child ready to take on new academic and social opportunities outside of your intimate circle of family and friends. The introduction of new media and technology in her early childhood should be carefully planned in order to support, not hinder, your child's development.

Your child needs to begin with hands-on learning experiences to develop the skills necessary to achieve healthy development. During her first years, new media use and technology should be very limited because they are not the ideal kinds of stimulus and they may interfere with important interactions. Once your child becomes more oriented to the world she can gradually be introduced to the digital universe. She will still need human interaction and real world activities to be her primary method of learning. Media literacy, which involves an important repertoire of competencies and knowledge related to media use, analysis and creation, will need to be taught to your child as she begins to engage with these new kinds of media. Digital devices and new media will eventually become an integrated part of your child's academic and social life, but she will need guidance to develop true mastery. The *Hierarchy of Media Use* is a guide for introducing new media in this gradual and developmentally-appropriate method.

THE HIERARCHY OF MEDIA USE:

MEDIA USE HIERARCHY		
Media	**Age Range for Introduction**	**Explanation**
Recorded Music	Birth	Music helps to soothe babies and to develop emotional regulation. Media devices can be used to provide a variety of recorded music, but make sure you stay in charge of digital devices until your child is old enough to use all of their functions appropriately.
Books	Birth (ebooks: 2-5) (Multimedia ebooks: 5+)	Babies can benefit from reading time from a very early age. Ebooks can be introduced around two or three with supervision, but are most beneficial if an adult is still reading them to your child. Multimedia ebooks/magazines and recorded books are too distracting and advanced for preschoolers.
Interactive Educational Games (apps, video/ computer	3-5	This can include creative games that involve painting drawing or making music, which are educational at this age

games)		because they allow children to develop some fine motor skills. It is important to note that drawing and writing with actual utensils is even more important and should not be replaced. Touchscreen apps are a great place to start because young children have the ability to pinch and touch well before they can click or type.
Educational Movies and Shows with no commercials	3-4	Educational cartoons attempt to incorporate an interactive quality by asking questions and encouraging children to respond. Other shows can introduce different cultures and explore topics related to science, art or history. Younger children still confuse fiction and reality, especially in live-action representations (anything not animated) and their screen time should be more limited so they can continue to develop skills through hands-on play. Also keep in mind that most children will struggle to follow

		many TV/Movie plots until they are 9 or 10. Just because they watch a show does not mean that they are following the story or understanding the intended messages.
Games and TV for entertainment (little or no educational value)	7-8	Other games and TV shows will become more accessible to this age group, but they should still contain age-appropriate content and promote positive values.
TV with commercials	7-9	Around age 7 children can begin to learn about advertising and the techniques used to "trick" people into thinking about and wanting products. Once your child has developed media literacy related to advertising, she can begin to think critically about commercials. Even with these tools, its better to avoid commercials when possible because they can still have a powerful effect on your child's thoughts and preferences.
Messaging (Email, texting,	8-11	Early messaging experiences should be

chats)		fully supervised by a parent and should not occur within a social media context which requires additional media literacy and maturity. Putting off texting and messaging may help your child to develop formal writing skills before they start using text lingo. Kids will eventually need to learn to move fluidly between different languages (text, casual, formal written English) as they navigate many different communication outlets. Parents and teachers can facilitate this by discussing the importance of context and by allowing children to become proficient at a language before they take on two more. It's okay for your child to let her friend know she will bbl (be back later), but you also want her to be able to spell it out when she needs to.
Internet Use	7 (supervised) 9-10 (monitored)	Children can begin to watch you navigate the internet at a young age, but should not be set free

		(even with supervision) until they are 9-10 and they have completed some basic media literacy training. Your child is not able to fully understand the concept of a global network and the way the internet functions until they are about 13 years old.
Social Media	12-15	Responsible social media use requires a complex understanding of the internet and it's potential which is not usually seen in children under the age of 13. Most social media sites also have a minimum age requirement of 13. Teen users will also need to have a fluent understanding of relevant media literacy concepts so they can make good decisions about the many complex social situations they may face when using this media.

Description and Explanations of Media

MUSIC

Recorded music is the only digital media experience recommended for babies. It should be combined with opportunities for live musical experiences including singing, drumming and other music making experiences. Music can help babies develop emotional regulation.[xi] Early on it can be used to soothe and relax your baby. It also encourages your baby to listen, move, dance and develop motor skills. In fact, early musical experiences may actually stimulate brain development. A recent study showed that one year olds who participated in interactive music lessons with a parent had more advanced social, communication and musical skills.[xii] These finding were only found in the babies who participated in interactive lessons with their parents, not those who were listening passively. This underscores how important parental engagement is at this stage. Babies and even toddlers learn best when they experience hands on learning that involves interaction with caregivers. Playing music for your child is great, but making music together with real or makeshift instruments or singing and dancing along with your child could be even more beneficial.

Music is also a great way to help young ones transition between activities. Initially a lullaby or song can be used to help signal bedtime. Other songs or music can be used as part of your child's routine to help transition from playtime to bath time or other activities. Think about the songs about cleaning up you may have heard if you have ever been to a preschool. These kinds of songs are used because they are developmentally appropriate and helpful for getting children to shift focus and transition to new activities.

Educational Benefits
- Develops Emotional Regulation (ability to manage emotions and behavior)
- Encourages Language Development
- There are many more benefits that can come from active music making and lessons

BOOKS

Books can be introduced as soon as possible and will help with early language development. In the beginning your child benefits from listening to your voice, hearing new words and developing a positive association with books. Reading together also helps your child develop early literacy skills and an interest in learning. Children will not begin engaging with the pictures or words in books until they are one to two years old. Ebooks can be introduced around two or three with supervision, but are most beneficial if they are read with an adult. Multimedia ebooks/magazines and recorded books are better for older children, because toddlers are still learning about books and learning to follow the sequence of the story. The narrative in a book can be interrupted if it is too complicated or has multimedia elements which can interfere with your child's comprehension.

Educational Benefits
- Develop Language skills
- Develop concepts about symbolism and written language
- Help improve attention span and concentration
- Encourages curiosity and a love of learning

EDUCATIONAL GAMES & APPS

Educational games or Apps can offer an additional source for learning and practicing new concepts and skills. Games have a more interactive quality because they require input and provide feedback. This can make them good tools for learning. The instantaneous feedback provided in games, whether it is sounds, images, prizes or points also commands attention and appeals to the pleasure center in our brains, which is why they can also become a little addictive. Very simple educational games may be appropriate for younger children and games that require more advanced strategy and creativity can support growth in older children. It is important to note that some manufacturers make educational claims that may be unfounded and not all games are appropriately rated. New touch screen technology and devices have made games more accessible to younger children, but future research will be required to assess how to make quality games and apps that truly support learning and achievement.

Educational Benefits

The educational benefits of early childhood games and especially apps, are still being studied and are not yet fully understood.

- Increased repetition of new concepts could increase learning
- May develop hand-eye coordination and fine motor skills
- Musical or artistic games could stimulate imagination and creativity

MOVIES AND TV SHOWS

For our purposes TV shows will include all shows, whether they were made for TV, internet or media streaming. There are three categories of shows that have different purposes and benefits.

1) Educational Movies and Shows with no commercials
2) Movies and Shows (with no commercials) for Entertainment
3) TV with commercials

Educational shows have been specifically designed to teach specific skills or knowledge and are created for all ages. Most shows designed for early childhood are meant to be educational, but not all of them provide proven learning benefits. A few quality shows developed in collaboration with educational and developmental experts have been shown to support early learning. Educational shows can be beneficial at any age though, and children who continue to watch more educational shows versus shows for entertainment tend to have increased academic achievement. However, children who are exposed to television too early may be more likely to develop problems with attention and learning challenges.

Movies and shows that contain no commercials or advertising are also more accessible and appropriate for younger children. The effects of advertising on children's food choices, eating habits and material preferences and requests has been well researched and can be very powerful. Around age seven children can begin to learn media literacy concepts that can help them understand the techniques that advertisers use to influence and manipulate people. This can help them be a little more guarded and skeptical of the messages presented. However, even with this knowledge, children and even adults can be very influenced by advertising.

Viewing shows that contain commercials should be reserved for older children and adults. The advertisements presented can have a powerful influence on your child and may present or promote messages and values that are unhealthy or do not fit with your family belief system. Commercials may also contain content that is not necessarily age-appropriate, even if the show your child is watching has an appropriate age-rating.

Educational Benefits
- Quality Early Childhood shows may teach early literacy skills and concepts
- Can teach about social skills, relationships and morality
- Develop knowledge of new subjects related to science, geography, culture, languages, diversity, history and literature

Shows that are not meant to be educational may contain misinformation, humor or satire which can confuse children and teach the wrong kind of messages.

VIDEO GAMES FOR ENTERTAINMENT
Video games including computer games and apps are a significant source of entertainment for many children. In elementary and middle school they can become an important part of a child's social culture and are a means for socializing and group play. Many children will interact with other players and friends via multiplayer games and they can develop strong social networks within a gaming

community. While this may be an important social outlet
for some, children need to be knowledgeable and mature
enough to manage online interactions before they
participate in games with this potential. Parents should
provide some supervision for this kind of activity and
discuss these relationships and interactions with their child
because they are very likely to run into bullying and
inappropriate or adult content and behavior. Initial
research shows that video game play may provide some
cognitive benefits, but games need to be age-appropriate
and game play should be limited so that other important
activities are not limited or excluded.

Educational Benefits

- Some research suggests that strategy games may
  increase cognitive flexibility[xiii]
- Action games can develop spatial skills and
  attention allocation ability[xiv]
- May enhance creative capacity[xv]
- Cooperative play may develop social skills and
  may also reduce aggression associated with violent
  video game play[xvi]

MESSAGING

There are now many forms of digital messaging
including texting, emailing and other chat/app or
message services. Most of this communication occurs on
devices that easily connect to the internet and social
media and much of it actually occurs online. Your child
should possess the appropriate media literacy and
maturity for internet and social media use before
participating in online messaging services. Messaging

friends becomes an important part of socializing for preteens and teenagers and may also be a good way for them to keep in communication with parents and family members.

INTERNET & SOCIAL MEDIA

Children may begin supervised internet use at a younger age, especially for school but they are not able to fully understand it's potential, and potential hazards, until they are teenagers. Even teens, who are notoriously impulsive, will likely make some poor choices related to internet and social media use and need continued guidance. Internet use has been linked to increased academic achievement in some scenarios and will eventually become an important part of school and homework. Social media use including media sharing involves a more complex understanding of the internet and advanced social skills. It also offers the potential to open children up to cyber-bullying and even more exposure to inappropriate content and behavior. It is important to remember that giving your child access to the internet is like letting them loose into the world. They can easily and unintentionally be exposed to extremist views, graphic violence, pornography, racism and other forms of prejudice and hate. Internet use should be fully supervised in the beginning and then intermittently monitored and discussed with teenagers. Parents should expect to discuss inappropriate content, cyber-bullying and other uncomfortable experiences with their child.

Educational Benefits

- Rich source for knowledge and educational content
- Offers potential for creativity, social interaction and cooperative learning

Chapter Summary

- Children need to learn basic concepts through hands-on learning experiences before they are introduced to educational media
- Early media use should be primarily educational
- Introduction of new media and devices should involve related media literacy lessons to promote
- responsible use

Ch. 4
Hierarchy of Responsibility and Independence

"True teachers are those who use themselves as bridges over which they invite their students to cross; then, having facilitated their crossing, joyfully collapse, encouraging them to create their own."
-Nikos Kazantzakis

Most people have had the experience of losing track of time when surfing the internet or playing a video game or app. Did you know that a three second distraction, such as checking a text message, doubles the amount of mistakes we make in our work?[xvii] There are many things about technology use that most adults are just discovering and figuring out how to manage. Unfortunately we often learn the hard way that mismanaging our media use can have

61

costly effects. We then have to learn or relearn skills to appropriately manage our time and attention. With your help, your child may be able to enter into adulthood with this knowledge and these skills already intact, so that he can maintain his health and wellbeing and still be an extremely productive person.

Developing the self-control, awareness and skills to self-monitor media use will be an essential competency for today's youth. Self-control and responsibility are things that can be taught and earned along the way, especially when it comes to media use. If this is done well, your child may have a significant advantage over others who did not grow up learning how to resist the addictive powers of technology. Most people struggle to figure out how to appropriately integrate technology into their lives. Like many things, it can be easier to learn these skills early on. Although technology will continue to evolve and change the world we live in, a good foundation of self-control, awareness and critical thinking will help your child navigate future experiences. These skills will most certainly provide an important advantage that will contribute to your child's success.

As with all things, your child will need to gradually learn how to appropriately self-monitor his media use at a developmentally appropriate pace. Very early on children do not have any of the skills or capabilities required to take on this task and need strict parental structure and guidance. This stage is essential, not only to protect your child from misuse, but to set appropriate expectations and to practice transitioning activities. Even adults have difficulty stopping sometimes because of the inherently addictive quality of digital media. As your child begins to develop awareness, the use of warnings can prepare him to take on some responsibility. With increased awareness and self-control he can begin to participate in adhering to parental guidelines and can work towards using other forms of assistance to help keep track of his behavior and use, thereby earning some freedom and responsibility. Older children will eventually be able to collaborate with parents to set appropriate boundaries, strategies and consequences for mistakes. This will mark the beginning of your child's opportunity to really increase awareness and to develop essential critical thinking skills by negotiating ideas with you. Eventually, teenagers can take on most of the responsibility for self-monitoring media use. Open-ended communication with parents and sporadic monitoring will still be important to help your child bridge the gap from dependent to fully independent. This stage allows teens to continue to learn from their mistakes and practice still-developing critical thinking skills which will help them make good choices as adults.

What are the Skills & Abilities Your Child will need to achieve Media Mastery?

- Strong Executive Functioning Skills (these involve the brain's ability to control thinking processes and supervise attention systems)
- Critical Thinking Skills- including the ability to be curious and critical about media messages and their purpose
- Awareness of the influence and kinds of distraction different media can create
- Knowledge about health effects related to inappropriate media use or overuse

- The ability to set boundaries around media use at home and school/work to counteract unwanted effects
- Knowledge about tips and tools for easily maintaining boundaries and keeping track of time and focus

Critical Thinking

Critical thinking is the ability to gather and assess evidence and information, and use clear reasoning methods to reach justified conclusions.

The 6 Critical Questions to Ask are:

Who- Who said it?

What- What kinds of facts or opinions are stated?

Where- Where was the information presented and what was the audience?

When- When or in what time context was the information presented?

Why- What was the motivation for presenting this information?

How- What media was used? What was the associated mood or tone?

Executive Functions

The executive functions are a set of processes that all have to do with managing oneself and one's resources in order to achieve a goal. It is an umbrella term for the neurologically-based skills involving mental control and self-regulation.

While there is no universally accepted comprehensive list of executive functions, they generally include:[xviii]

- **Inhibition** - the ability to stop one's own behavior

at the appropriate time, including stopping actions and thoughts

- **Shift** - the ability to move freely from one situation to another and to think flexibly in order to respond appropriately to the situation
- **Emotional Control** - the ability to modulate emotional responses by bringing rational thought to bear on feelings
- **Initiation** - the ability to begin a task or activity and to independently generate ideas, responses, or problem-solving strategies
- **Working memory** - the capacity to hold information in mind for the purpose of completing a task
- **Planning/Organization** - the ability to manage current and future-oriented task demands
- **Organization of Materials** - the ability to impose order on work, play, and storage spaces
- **Self-Monitoring** - the ability to monitor one's own performance and to measure it against some standard of what is needed or expected

Early Media Literacy Goals & Age Ranges

Level	Developmental Age-Range	Goals
New Users	0-6	1. Practice talking about the media they are using including identifying different kinds of media and devices and expressing preferences and thoughts about content

		2. Identifying when and where media use is allowed, such as after dinner or during TV-time at home 3. Learning to be careful with media devices and treat them with respect 4. Learning when and how media time ends
Transitional Users	5-7	1. Discussing media content including what happens and how they feel about different content and media 2. Developing comprehension skills for different kinds of media including reading, video and listening comprehension 3. Develop knowledge about how media impacts them including emotional impact and basic health effects, such as making it hard to fall asleep. 4. Learning to adhere to media time limits and transition to new activities
Intermediate	7-10	1. Ability to

		discuss and begin analyzing media content with others
		2. Discuss the purpose of media content including whether it is for entertainment or learning, what messages it shares, and why it might have been created
		3. Continue to expand knowledge of how media impacts them, including individual differences and feelings, such as this particular game makes me feel frustrated
		4. Participate in self-monitoring media time limits with assistance of parents and tools (such as timers)

The *Responsible and Independent Media Use Hierarchy* below provides loose guidelines for moving your child towards responsible independent media use as adults. All children develop different skills and abilities according to their own timeline, so it will be important to keep your child's strengths and skills in mind. Expecting too much or even expecting too little from him can cause frustration, disappointment and impair development in these areas. Some initial frustration and challenges are normal, but you may need to adjust your pace or strategy if you and your child continue to struggle at any point.

STAGES OF RESPONSIBLE AND INDEPENDENT MEDIA USE

Routine and Redirection (0-4)

Media use should be very limited during this time. Your child has no ability to determine what kind of and how much media use is right for him. He may let you know he's had enough by moving on to another activity. If he has had too much exposure or too much sedentary time he may let you know by getting cranky or irritable. Do not be fooled just because your child shows interest in something, this does not necessarily mean it's an age-appropriate choice for him or that it isn't time to move on to something else. It is most important for children this age to be exploring the world around them and engaging in multi-sensory play.

Complete Parental Monitoring with Warnings (3-6)

Your child will begin developing the concept of time during this stage, but will initially have no real understanding of it. This is significant because it is still very important to limit the amount of time he spends with technology, especially screen media. Time warnings will help your child learn about the concept of time and can help him begin to appreciate how time can go quickly when you are engaged with media devices.

Parental Monitoring and Assistance (6-12)

It is during this stage that your child will make significant advances in his thinking and reasoning abilities which will allow him to begin learning more about how media can affect his life. This is a critical time to begin teaching him media literacy lessons because media will become a more integrated part of his daily life. He will be ready to take on more responsibility for following family guidelines for his media use, but he will still need lots of parental guidance so he can learn about and practice his media literacy and critical thinking skills.

Collaborative Planning and Decision Making (11-15)

Preteens will begin declaring their independence and will also become even more involved in using media as a part of their social lives. It is critical that parents continue to stay involved in offering guidance because this is when they will most likely begin using the most complex forms of media which require the greatest amount of knowledge and caution. Using discussion and collaborative planning is key to staying connected with your child as he navigates the increasingly complex terrain of social media.

Open-Ended Communication & Periodic Monitoring (14-18)

Teenagers need to make significant advances in their ability to independently self-monitor their media use, because they will soon be considered adults with full access to the world and the responsibility of adult consequences. Parents can participate by keeping communication open with teenagers so that they can help them adapt and learn from their mistakes.

RESPONSIBLE AND INDEPENDENT MEDIA USE HIERARCHY		
STAGE	AGE RANGE	INSTRUCTIONS
Routine and Redirection	0-4	Young children are especially likely to struggle with transitions from stimulating activities and they have little to no concept of time. The use of redirection (distracting attention to another activity) and using natural endings and conclusions can help with this. **Example of Redirection**- use music or songs to signal transition to the next activity or introduce a planned drink or snack to end media time **Examples of Natural Endings**- Set a game to end at 10 minutes (or device to turn off) or play a 20 minutes show and turn off right at the end. These proactive steps can save both you and your child a lot of energy and potential frustration.
Complete Parental Monitoring With Warnings	3-6	All media should be carefully chosen and monitored by parents. Explicitly discuss time limits and schedules with your child and provide warnings to prepare your child for transitions when appropriate.

		Examples- Provide 5 and 1 minute time warnings; Set a timer and show your child how screen time will end when the timer beeps
Parental Monitoring & Assistance	6-12	School-aged children are ready to begin taking on some responsibility for their media use, but guidelines for media use should still be set by parents. Allow your child to set the timer and/or turn off devices themselves, but expect him/her to need continued reminders. Choices related to new games or shows and media content should be discussed, but decisions should ultimately be made by parents. **Example-** Download a game timer app and use it to help your child turn off the device after the allotted time. **Hint-** Routines are still important. Building entertainment time into your child's schedule can help set expectations and make it easier to stop and move on to the next activity.
Collaborative Planning and Decision Making	11-15	Allow pre-teens and teens to participate in discussing and creating their own limits and schedules for screen-time and

		digital media. Parents should still be involved in helping them make appropriate choices and regularly monitoring and discussing content, especially as social media becomes a part of their life.
Open-Ended Communication & Periodic Monitoring	14-18	Teenagers are more than ready to announce their independence and take control of their own habits and media use, but parents can still provide helpful guidance. By keeping up open-ended communication with your teen and being involved in his digital life, you can provide guidance and help him think critically about the choices he makes. Expect your teen to make some mistakes along the way, but use these opportunities to have a discussion so you can help him learn better ways to use media in the future.

Additional Advantages of Responsible Use

One of the greatest benefits of developing responsible media use habits at a young age is that it can help build executive functioning skills and abilities that are essential for overall success in all areas of independent functioning. It may actually counteract many concerns related to media use including those related to deficits in executive functioning skills, attention, patience and academic performance. Screen media are associated with alterations in children's developing attentional system. We know that early exposure to television during critical periods of brain development is associated with subsequent attentional problems. Children who watch television before they are 4 years old have a significantly increased risk of developing attention problems by the time they are 7.[xix] While early exposure appears to be the most critical, all children who exceed screen-time recommendations have up to two-times more likelihood of having significant attention deficits.[xx] Your child is born with the potential for executive function, but the skills themselves have to be developed and taught. Practicing responsible media use requires and helps develop executive functioning skills including inhibition, planning, emotional control and self-monitoring.

Knowledge about the effects of media use and appropriate planning and scheduling of media time can also prevent immediate disadvantages related to specific media use. Short-term effects of television and computer game use include inferior verbal memory performance and trouble sleeping.[xxi] The part of your child's brain that control's emotional responsiveness is also impacted by violent video games. This creates a temporary tendency towards more aggressive behavior immediately after playing these games.[xxii] A child who develops appropriate media literacy knowledge and responsible use patterns can avoid these kind of effects because he will learn to plan and coordinate media use so that it does not interfere with his attitude and performance on other activities. This kind of forethought and planning is of course very dependent on strong executive functioning skills which are continuing to develop even into early adulthood. Your child will need your guidance to make these kinds of decisions and to learn to prioritize his health and performance.

Developing boundaries related to using media intentionally and at appropriate times can fend off some of the distraction factors associated with new technology. Strong executive functioning skills and a practice of focusing his full attention on important tasks can prevent poor habits of multitasking while learning. Research shows that multitasking actually changes the way that you learn and the parts of the brain used in learning and remembering. When people are not distracted they are more likely to fully utilize parts of the brain which are meant for storing and recalling information.[xxiii] This is one way that good media habits can improve academic performance.

Children who watch modest amounts of television and those that watch more educational programming also have higher achievement test scores.[xxiv] Research findings offer strong indications that media content, including the intent, messages and educational value, play a strong part in determining the overall impact of media.[xxv] This suggests even more reason to emphasize making informed choices about media and to discuss media content with your child. Even if you had doubts about the benefits of helping your child develop his own responsible media use habits, there is clear evidence that children whose parents monitor their media use and discuss media content and limits with them have more positive health and social outcomes and increased academic performance.[xxvi]

Chapter Summary

- Developing self-control, awareness and critical thinking related to media use can help your child become a responsible user of technology
- Your child will need your help to learn and practice strategies for managing media use responsibly and he may continue to struggle with this into his teen years
- The skills and abilities for responsible technology use could counteract many concerns related to media use

PART II: AGE SPECIFIC GUIDELINES

Ch. 5
0-2 Avoiding the Screen

*"I would teach children music, physics, and philosophy; but most
importantly music, for the patterns in music and all the arts are the
keys to learning."*
-Plato

Developmental Priorities
☐ Language Development
☐ Basic Problem-Solving Skills
☐ Learning to walk and jump
☐ Developing manual dexterity
☐ Learning about emotions and self-soothing
☐ Learning to play with other children
☐ Developing a sense of self

Now is the time to introduce old media. Children under the age of three should not be regularly introduced to screen media such as TV, computers, tablets or smart phones. The term avoid will be used because in the modern era it would be almost impossible and certainly impractical for most families to completely escape exposure. Incidental exposure will absolutely happen, especially if you allow your child to leave your home at any point during his first three years of life. There may also be instances where you determine that minimal use, such as a FaceTime chat with a family member, could offer more potential benefit than harm. Avoid simply means you should not intentionally introduce your child to the world of screen media until he is a little bit older. Your child does not need it and there is no evidence that he will benefit from these forms of media use. There are other forms of media that are great for babies and toddlers, such as recorded music. Traditional print media including picture and children's books are also excellent resources. Remember that everything is new to your baby. You will need to start from the beginning and work towards more advanced technology use.

How Does Background TV Affect Your Child?

A TV playing in the background can impair your child's ability to focus on his own play. In one study, children ages 1-3 were observed during a one-hour play session with background TV. Researchers noted that these children's play episodes were shorter, less complex, and included less focused attention than when the television was not on.[xxvii] This is significant because your child's play is a very

---

important developmental task that promotes learning and
growth.

American Academy of Pediatrics Guidelines

The American Academy of Pediatrics currently
recommends no digital media use for children from birth
to 18 months and discourages solo use until at least age 2.
Even at two years of age they recommend only high
quality educational media and suggest parents continue
coviewing until age 5. These guidelines are meant to be
shared with parents by all pediatricians, but unfortunately
they are widely unknown or ignored by many parents and
educators. There is still some controversy surrounding
these guidelines with experts both suggesting that they are
in some ways too restrictive and also too lenient. The
critical time for brain growth is actually in the first three
years of life and many studies have pointed to negative
effects for two-year-olds, especially related to passive
screen viewing time. The AAP's current guidelines have
been recently update to try to incorporate new media use
patterns such as video-chatting and the use of apps. The
AAP recognizes that the current norm for early childhood
media use does not fit within their guidelines. There is a
legitimate fear that if guidelines appear too strict or
challenging then they will be completely ignored. There
have also been instances where these guidelines have been
misunderstood to mean that any exposure to screens
causes damage. There is no known harm caused by single
exposure to screen media. Health concerns are primarily
related to repeat exposure, such as daily use or distraction
caused by frequent adult use.

A baby's environment is still for the most part within the control of his parents and should be modified to create the safest and healthiest option available. It is common practice to baby-proof your home to avoid known physical hazards for children. Most families already make adjustments in their functioning, such as keeping quiet while baby is sleeping and arranging schedules around nap time. Creating a media-safe environment in your home for your baby is only an extension of this concept. It will be up to each individual family to determine how to implement the best options for your home and family.

Ideas for Screen-Proofing Your Home	
Make Social Areas Social	Keep Screen Media like TVs and computers in more private places like a bedroom, study or separate TV room, so that older family members can privately enjoy screen time when they are not directly caring for your baby or toddler. This can benefit the whole family because it encourages more undistracted social interaction and removes background media which affects everyone, not just baby.
Protect all Devices	Keep smartphones and tablets out of reach by storing and charging them in adult-only places, such as an office or on a tall piece of furniture. If your child cannot see or reach these things while playing, they won't be as tempted. Once you allow your child to play with these devices, it becomes harder to keep them off limits.
Create a Guest Charging	This can encourage guests and other caregivers to also keep their devices protected and away from your child.

Station	
Invest in a Modern Stereo System	Keep this available in your home in case you want to catch a sports game or enjoy some adult entertainment outside of nap time. You can always use the radio or plug in your smartphone and listen to a podcast. Having this available may also remind or encourage you to listen to music with your child. Just remember to also keep it somewhere out of reach, especially if you are going to plug your smartphone into it.
Have Special Toys and Activities Available	Keep a few toys or activities special by only offering them to your child at certain times. You can use these, instead of screen media devices, to offer a brief distraction for your child when you really need it. Quiet toys and activities are especially great for this, such as glitter wands, playdough and puzzles.

Learning Experiences for Babies & Toddlers

Early experiences with music, reading, and active play provide known benefits for very young children. Listening to music can help with your child's language development as well as emotional regulation. Musical play and making music together with a caregiver has been shown to provide the most benefit including advances in social and communication skills. Singing, dancing and listening to music with your child are also great learning experiences. This could involve music from an iPod or other digital device. It is also great entertainment for car rides.

Reading to your baby and toddler has long been promoted as a significant learning experience to assist with language development and early literacy skills. Board books and picture stories are a great place to start and the length and complexity of books can increase as your child's attention span increases.

Active play time is your child's primary learning activity during early childhood and is how he will develop the physical, cognitive, social and emotional skills he will need to begin formal education. Your child will naturally engage in this kind of play but you can support him by providing safe age-appropriate toys and by engaging in play with him. Interactive play will support his social and emotional development and can be an invaluable opportunity for you to support your child's growth. If you encourage and support your child when he struggles with a task during play, even if it's just learning to open the toy box, you can help your child develop the patience and frustration tolerance he will need to take on future challenges.

Healthy Screen Media Alternatives		
AGE	**INTERACTIVE PLAY**	**FREE PLAY**
0-12 months	Talk to your baby and respond to him Show him how to turn the pages in a book and point out animals and other pictures Sing and dance with your child Roll a ball with your child or pick up items so that your child can drop them	Offer safe toys and items for your child to taste, touch, shake and listen to Play music for your child to listen to Allow your child to begin to explore his environment through movement with jumpers and push toys

12-24 months	Sing and play songs that your child can sing along to, especially songs with rhymes Read short books to your child (repetition is good and your child may want to read the same book over and over) Model simple activities for your child and then let him have a try (drawing, pouring, stirring, opening a box)	Provide toys that imitate real life like plastic food, animals and even cleaning accessories Provide sensory experiences such as sand and water play with cups and bowls for filling (this may require closer supervision) Finger painting, drawing and playdough Give your child boxes and containers to put things in or shape sorter toys
24-36 months	Play musical games such as "freeze" and the hokey pokey or show your child how to use instruments Create art with your child (show him how to trace his hands and feet) or allow him to help you cook by stirring and pouring Teach your child to throw or kick a ball (catching may come later) Continue to read to him	Introduce simple puzzles Provide more opportunities for your child to play with others Allow your child to play with and read picture books on his own Provide props for imaginative play including dress up items Continue providing sensory play experiences

		Drawing, coloring or painting

Real-world Challenges

TV time, tablets and smartphones are often given to children to entertain them, keep them quiet in a challenging situation, and to give parents a break. Raising a child and taking care of a family is a lot of work and all parents need a moment sometimes. You may also encounter judgment from others and experience embarrassment in public when your children act like real babies and toddlers. Most places are not 100% child-friendly and constantly supervising, being safety enforcer, and trying to appease others around you is exhausting. Technology often becomes a quick fix tool to make life a little easier. This is after all the purpose of technology, to make our lives a little easier. The problem with some of these choices and habits is that the long-term costs can out way short-term benefits. Children have always acted like children. Most parenting challenges haven't changed, even if they look a little different now. Working through these challenges is an important learning experience for children and parents, because it requires growth in areas such as patience, attention, and emotional regulation. These are things that need to gradually be negotiated between parent and child and are not just skills for your child to develop. All parents need to continue to cultivate their own patience, tolerance for discomfort and creativity in this relationship. This allows you to grow as a parent and offer the immense amount of guidance and support that your child will need throughout their childhood. The landscape of parenting is ever changing and as soon as you get comfortable and help your child master one challenge, he will be on to something new. It is helpful to get comfortable with the idea of being uncomfortable.

How Does TV Impact Your Parenting?

A study that examined parent-child interaction when a TV was on in the room found that parents were less engaged and less involved with their children.[xxviii] This was surprising because parents were instructed to play with their child and knew that they were being observed. In a real world setting, TV is likely to be an even bigger distraction. Remember that quality parent-child interaction is essential to your child's brain development.

If you allow your child to engage in self-directed play at an early age, this will become a comfortable skill for him and will ultimately benefit both of you. Children who engage in more free play are better at creative problem solving, develop more self-confidence, and are motivated to learn. They also require less attention and guidance from parents. If your child has these skills, you can be free to supervise without providing constant entertainment for your child. Many children these days struggle with self-directed play because they have not been encouraged to explore on their own and because distractions like TV actually discourage this behavior. If your child struggles with self-directed play, give it time, this is a skill that he can learn. You may need to help him at first by providing encouragement and introducing open-ended play opportunities. Helping your child discover how to play and be curious is likely to provide much more benefit long-term than anything introduced on TV or in a game.

Toys to Encourage Open-Ended Play	
AGE TO INTRODUCE	
0-9 months	Mobiles Rattles Sensory Blankets Pop-up books and toys Simple Blocks Balls Stuffed Animals
9-18 months	Crayons Cars and Trucks Dolls Musical Instruments Finger Paint Cups, Bowls, Boxes and Containers Plastic Food and other pretend items Plastic animals and figures (large enough to avoid choking hazards) Pillows and Blankets
18-36 months	Costumes and Dress Up Clothes Painting with Brushes Markers Stickers Chalk or Dry Erase Boards Building Blocks Dollhouses Puppets

**Toys that have buttons or "do" things, do not encourage open-ended play

---

Tips for Playing with Your Child

1. Allow your child to take the lead
2. Allow your child to struggle a little and to figure things out on his own
3. Be playful and match your child's curiosity and enthusiasm
4. For more information on specific play stages from 0-3 check out this free resource: *The Power of Play: Learning through Play from Birth to Three* at www.zerotothree.org

---

Benefits of Screen Free Time for Parents

Parents can also benefit from reducing screen time for themselves and their children. Health concerns related to overuse of digital media are not limited to children. Technology use is also frequently a distraction that keeps us from being present in the moment and reduces the quality of engagement with the people around you. The simple act of being present in the moment can have enormous benefit both for you and the people around you, especially your children. Mindfulness and "being present" has been well researched and has been shown to improve people's mental health and sense of wellbeing.[xxix] All caregivers need to take care of themselves in order to perform at their best and provide loving care.

Concerns related to media overload in adults include:
- Increases in sleep disorders, stress and depression[xxx]

- Difficulties related to relaxing and recovering at the end of the day[xxxi]
- Increase in selfish behavior and decreased social consciousness[xxxii]
- Reduced capacity for cognitive processes (thinking, memory) due to frequent distraction[xxxiii]

The Myth of Multitasking

Do you use technology to multitask?
What we often think of as multitasking is impossible in most situations and actually involves *task-switching* which actually reduces our productivity and can sometimes diminish the quality of work completed.[xxxiv] Recent research suggests that people who believe they are excellent multitaskers are usually worse at completing multiple tasks and often have difficulty with impulsivity and concentration.[xxxv]

What about 2 year olds?

Two-year-olds are still within the same critical developmental stage as babies and one-year-olds, so you may want to continue the "avoid passive screen exposure" guideline until your child turns three. This is a cautious approach which seeks to avoid harm, especially where no or only limited potential benefit can be identified. You may decide that for your child and your family some screen exposure would be beneficial. If this is the case, consider interactive media such as games or apps instead of TV or videos which are passive. It is also possible that new research will result in new educational media that offers potential benefits that may outweigh any potential harm at this age. If you do choose to expose your two-year-old to new media be sure to read through the recommendations in the next chapter to learn about age-appropriate options. Be very wary of any educational claims by manufacturers and make sure that the research used to back up claims has been published in a peer-reviewed journal or by a professional organization such as the American Academy of Pediatrics. Otherwise, you may be robbing your child of valuable real-world learning time. Any real-world exploration, play or positive human interaction is beneficial for a child this age. Media use should certainly be kept to a minimum and should not be a regular part of your child's daily routine at this stage. You should always avoid background TV exposure, because this is certainly not beneficial and repeated exposure may cause long-term harm.

0-2 Year Old Guidelines	
*Do not introduce screen media into your child's daily routine until they are at least 2 years old	
Beneficial Media Experiences	Print media including baby books, picture books and reading time Music including digitally recorded music; Singing along and dancing with your child may have increased benefit (be sure to also encourage music making with simple instruments)
Experiences to Avoid	Avoid background television which can affect your child's attention and negatively impact important play and learning activities Keep digital devices such as smart phones out of reach of young children; When they are ready to use these you

will want them to learn to treat them with respect and to use them appropriately, which may be difficult if they have already been introduced as toys

Try to keep your own digital media use to a minimum when you are directly supervising or engaging with your child because this can negatively impact important bonding time and relationship feedback which affects your child's brain development

Chapter Summary

- Avoid introducing screen media, especially TV, into your baby or toddler's routine
- Introduce music and books to your child
- Encourage your child to engage in independent free play
- Spend some quality time engaging in playful activities along with your child
- Consider extending your passive screen media avoidance until age 3

Ch. 6

3-4 Introducing Technology

"Our children are only as brilliant as we allow them to be."
-Eric Michael Leventhal

Developmental Priorities

- ☐ Expand vocabulary and language skills
- ☐ Learn to count, sort and understand sequence and time
- ☐ Increasing curiosity and imagination
- ☐ Improve physical coordination including hand and finger skills
- ☐ Learn to cooperate and share with others
- ☐ Develop independence, self-esteem and empathy
- ☐ Using words to express needs and feelings

Your child has conquered walking and talking and now knows how to fully explore the world around her. At the age of 3 your child may be ready to learn about new media and technology. She may impress you with her easy grasp of touch screen technology, but remember she is just a beginner. She needs parental supervision as she learns about technology including careful monitoring and discussion of content. Even games or shows that are advertised as educational or kid friendly may not be appropriate for her at this age. You should be very wary of potential exposure to advertisements of any kind. At this stage you may have to rely on your own judgement and knowledge to determine if something is age-appropriate and reinforces your family values. To do this you need to have a good understanding of your child's developmental needs and abilities. Media content often misses the mark with this age group, because creators do not always understand very young children's cognitive skills. Even shows that promote a positive message can actually be a bad influence in ways that are unintentional and not necessarily obvious. Many educational shows or games will actually provide no educational benefit for this age. Being the media supervisor for your child may still be a lot of work at this point, so don't count on it to be an easy independent activity. Your child's media exposure should be limited at this stage anyway, because she has many other important activities to engage in. Her energy may be a good clue to suggest how much physical activity she needs. Her primary mode of learning still needs to be hands on real world experience including a lot of interpersonal interaction with caregivers and others.

What's the best early learning activity for your child?

Reading with your child is by far one of the most valuable activities to promote early literacy skills and an interest in learning. Highlighting characters from books can also be a good way to emphasize reading and keep your child interested. At this age you might consider decorating with or providing toys related to characters from books instead of cartoon characters from TV.

Beginner Technology

You may already be using technology to play music for your child and she should be familiar with some traditional print media (ie. books). So what is the next step? Ebooks are a good place to start, especially if you and your child already enjoy reading together. The novelty might also pique your child's interest and allow you to enjoy even more stories together. Ebooks also present an excellent opportunity to begin developing your child's media literacy. At this stage you want to help your child understand that media content refers to real world concepts. Simple ebooks can more easily be understood as a digital book. Three-year-olds are developing wild imaginations and still have difficulty distinguishing fantasy and reality, so it is important to introduce appropriate content that is not too frightening, even with books.

Interactive games such as computer games and apps might also interest your child, especially if they involve touch-screen technology. Keep in mind that computer mouses and other complex controllers might require a level of dexterity and coordination that your child does not yet have. The key here is the interactive quality of a game, because this is how young children learn. Games that request and provide immediate feedback will engage younger children. Look for games with buttons that make sounds and shorter actions such as jumping or sliding or moving objects versus games with complex goals or puzzles. It should be a game that your child can figure out with little intervention or help, otherwise she is missing out on an opportunity to develop her resilience and problem solving skills. You may realize that a game is not developmentally appropriate if your child is consistently wanting you to play it instead or asking you to complete actions for her. Generally she should be encouraged to figure out game play herself with verbal assistance and less hands on help. Improving at a game is also an opportunity to develop her sense of independence and self-esteem. Games or apps that are inappropriate or too challenging can defeat this purpose and actually hurt self-esteem. You should know and play around with any game that your 3-year-old plays.

You might also decide to allow your child to watch some preschool shows for entertainment. The best shows attempt to be interactive by directly addressing your child at times and encouraging participation or responses. These shows should always be pre-recorded and played without commercials. You may be able to play them from a DVD or Blu-Ray Disc or stream them from an internet provider so they don't have intermittent advertising. Recording live TV is not a great option, even if you fast-forward through the commercials for your child. At this age, commercials are detrimental in two ways. First and foremost, your child does not have the ability to interpret and analyze the messages being presented to her and is very influenced by them. She also does not have the ability to fully differentiate commercial and show or to follow a storyline through a commercial break. Even if you are fast-forwarding through commercials, her viewing experience and comprehension are likely to be disrupted. Keep in mind that watching these shows is still more about entertainment than education. Your child can learn about new things through educational shows, but she will still learn new concepts more quickly if they are presented in person. If you choose to introduce shows to your three-year-old, try to watch them with her and discuss them. This can increase any potential learning opportunity. She may also benefit from watching the same show over and over again.

While some media use may appear to be intuitive at a young age, it is not necessary for your child to begin using it this early. These skills can be learned at a later stage very easily and in a short period of time. In fact, if for practical or safety reasons you chose to keep technology away from your toddler for several more years, she would still quickly and easily be able to catch up to her peers when it becomes necessary for her to use technology in school or in her social life. Still, many parents find benefit in allowing very young children to use appropriate technology, whether it's for a 15-minute distraction or getting through the last few minutes of an adult-centered activity.

Currently there is no reason to completely avoid screen technology at this age, as long as the technology and it's content is age appropriate and it is used in moderation. Keep in mind that moderation and age appropriate content at this age may feel extremely limited compared to the average use and range of options for adults and older children. Make sure that you consider the context and purpose of your child's media use. Is your child using technology to fill otherwise unstimulating downtime or could she be doing something more active? Is your child playing this game or watching this show because it's educational? There are no wrong answers to these questions, but you do want to limit her screen time and also make it count for something whenever possible. Right now she doesn't need digital media to be a primary form of entertainment. It is very important that she spends most of her time in creative and imaginative play.

Media Literacy

Media Literacy is the ability to access, analyze, evaluate and create media in a variety of forms. Children need to develop media literacy skills to understand the messages constantly being delivered through mass media and so that they learn to use media appropriately.

Resources to help teach your child media literacy:
Center for Media Literacy
www.medialit.org
Media Literacy Project
www.medialiteracyproject.org
Powerful Voices for Kids
www.powerfulvoicesforkids.com

Responsible Use Guidelines

No matter what new media you introduce at this stage, a major goal should be helping your child learn to respect technology and expensive devices. Three-year-olds do not yet fully understand the value of money, but they are old enough to begin learning. Using technology and accessing new media should be a privilege, not a right. Even as an adult your child will have to earn the money and the opportunities to utilize technology. Misuse of any kind can have consequences at any age, so learning to be a responsible user is important. Your child is too young to take on very much responsibility for her technology use, but she can begin learning that it deserves some respect. You need to be fully responsible for monitoring her technology use and media exposure by supervising content and usage and enforcing time limits. At this age you will want to rely on following routines and using redirection to transition to different activities. Do not expect your child to easily stop playing with or watching something she is enjoying. Plan ahead to avoid potentially difficult transitions. Giving her more time and attention to helping her shift her focus can also prevent irritability and meltdowns. Try to keep screen time to less than an hour a day on most days. Your child should not be sedentary for more than an hour at a time at this age and two hours should be the maximum total screen time for one day.

Media to Avoid
- TV or shows with commercials
- Apps or Games with advertising
- Advergames- games that advertise a product or brand
- Media with violent content, even if it is unrealistic/cartoon violence
- Shows that demonstrate "bad" or immoral behavior without immediate consequences (3-year-olds cannot follow a complex story plot)

- Media with frightening characters or scenes
- Games with a rating other than *Early Childhood* (E is not actually for everyone)

Hints for determining if a show could be educational for your toddler

3-year-olds are mostly likely to learn from shows that:
- Have lots of sound effects
- Ask your child questions and let her think about simple choices
- Talk about colors, numbers or letters, and practice counting
- Talk about animals and wildlife
- Introduce cultures and places that your child has not been exposed to
- Encourage imagination
- Model positive behaviors such as sharing and helping others

Your child could learn negative behaviors from shows that demonstrate poor behavior without immediately addressing it. *This can be true even if a show has a story that attempts to show that unfriendly or poor behavior can have negative consequences.*

Are there quality educational shows, games and apps for my child?

Toddlers do not need digital media in their lives to learn and there are no studies that show that media use can improve their intelligence. Some games may allow children to continue working on important skills that they might otherwise be developing through traditional play activities, such as painting or drawing apps or games that involve discovery and imagination. You can also find games that teach colors, shapes and ABCs, but don't use this as a replacement for other learning. Not all of these concepts will transfer to early literacy skills. Quality educational shows such as Sesame Street, Blue's Clues and Dora the Explorer have been shown to offer some long-term benefit including increasing children's later academic performance and interest in education and reading. This has only been shown to be true for some quality educational programming. Many games and shows that claim to be educational have no evidence to backup their claims. In fact some educational shows have been shown to unintentionally promote poor behavior and understanding because, despite their advertising, they were not actually age-appropriate. Be wary of any current games, videos or interactive media that make claims about proven benefits for this age group. Your child may learn some new content (ie. shapes, colors) but digital learning will not make her smarter. While there are resources that can help highlight the age-appropriateness of media content, it is much more challenging to figure out if something is actually educational.

Most of the research on early childhood programming seems to demonstrate that age-appropriate educational TV provides more learning benefit than other TV or no intervention. Nothing has shown that these shows are more beneficial than the numerous other learning opportunities available to preschoolers, only that TV may be better than nothing. Using educational games and shows to fill some downtime could be beneficial but should not replace other kinds of learning. If you have the ability to offer your child other opportunities for learning including preschool and/or other extracurricular classes like art, music, dance or even your own one-on-one activity time, you should certainly take advantage of these things. Most communities offer many early learning experiences at places like nature centers, museums, festivals/fairs, or community centers. Remember that relationships are key to early childhood development and learning so any opportunity to learn from and enjoy the company of parents, adults and peers is invaluable.

Age 3-4 Guidelines	
Beginner Media	Ebooks Simple Games or Apps Shows without commercials *Continue providing music and books*
Time Limits	1 hour per day of screen time (2 hours maximum) Aim for short time periods like a 20 minute show or 15 minutes of game time to reduce sedentary time
Content Guidelines	Simple ebooks with lots of pictures Apps/Games that mimic play (painting, drawing, building) Games rated for Early Childhood Interactive Early Childhood shows without commercials Look for educational content Avoid violence and scary scenes or

	characters Avoid media that includes stereotypes and gender bias
Responsible Use	Make technology a privilege Teach your child to be careful with expensive devices Use Routine and Redirection to help your child transition to different activities

Resources for Media Content Reviews

CommonSenseMedia.org- offers reviews and age-based media recommendations for shows, games, books and movies

PBS.org/Parents- offers media recommendations based on developmental stages

Kidsfirst.org- rates and reviews movies, music, TV shows and games and endorses media that meets their KIDS FIRST! criteria

Chapter Summary

- You can introduce ebooks, simple games and educational shows to your three or four-year-old child
- Avoid shows and games with commercials and advertisements
- Limit screen media time to less than 2 hours a day
- Introduce media that is educational and does not have frightening scenes or characters

- Think about the purpose for your child's media use to make sure she is maximizing her time and energy for beneficial learning experiences

Creating personalized Guidelines for your 3 and 4 Year-Old

What new media will you introduce to your child?

When will you introduce it?

Who will be in charge of teaching your child about this technology?

What tools can you use to monitor your child's use?

How will you keep track of how much screen-media your child uses each day/week?

How will you make sure that other family member's media use does not expose your child to inappropriate content?

How will you and other family members demonstrate responsible media use for your child?

If you have older children, how will you make adjustments for their different needs? (see Chapter 10 for ideas)

Ch. 7
5-6 Transitional Users

"The more that you read, the more things you will know. The more you learn, the more places you'll go."
-Dr. Seuss, "I Can Read With My Eyes Shut!"

Developmental Priorities
- ☐ Develop more complex Communication Skills
- ☐ Analytical Thinking and Problem Solving
- ☐ Skills for Reading and Writing
- ☐ Beginner math concepts
- ☐ Sequencing and storytelling
- ☐ Advanced movement, coordination and Fine Motor Skills

- ☐ Developing Curiosity- Exploring how and why things happen
- ☐ Improve Social Skills and learn to maintain friendships
- ☐ Express feelings and develop sympathy and empathy
- ☐ Development of personal and family values

Your five or six-year-old will quickly develop skills to comfortably navigate new media devices. As a digital native, he may seem like an advanced user compared to older newbies. Do not be fooled by his apparent ease of use; he will still need parental supervision, support and media literacy lessons. A more complete knowledge and understanding of media content, use and functions is required to develop true mastery and conscientious use. This stage in his life will be full of learning and transitions as his body and mind are preparing for more advanced academic and social experiences. This can also be a time for your child to transition towards more regular media use, though he will still benefit from numerous real-world activities which promote his well-rounded development. Eventually an integrated use of media in his life is inevitable, and early lessons and experiences can prepare you both for this change. For now his media use should have clear limits, because he still needs to have more real-world interactions and experiences.

Children this age should be encouraged to spend as much time as possible practicing reading skills. Games, apps or ebooks that involve reading and writing skills can increase your child's reading exposure. Keep in mind that other kinds of media use could detract from important learning opportunities at this crucial stage in your child's education and put your child at risk of falling behind, especially as reading for comprehension becomes a core learning requirement. For example, television viewing during early elementary school has been shown to interfere with early reading.[xxxvi] You need to find an approach that is balanced and supports your child's individual needs. Some children will need more practice and encouragement to learn to read and even more support to find enjoyment in the possibilities that reading can offer.

Early Literacy Goals for 6 Year Olds

- Write their name
- Recognize all upper and lower case letters
- Speak in complete sentences
- Read and identify at least some words
- Sound out words when trying to spell
- Recall a story and answer open-ended questions about it

New Media and Technology

It's important to introduce new media and technology in a gradual and logical sequence. If your child has already begun reading ebooks, playing simple video games or apps, and watching educational shows, then he may be ready to explore more advanced media. He may now have enough physical skill to participate in new kinds of games, such as exergames or more fast-paced games. Be aware that research shows that providing exergames games to children does not increase overall physical activity and does not provide any significant health benefits.[xxxvii] These games cannot replace time spent in other forms of play and physical activity, but they may encourage development of specific motor skills including hand-eye or foot-eye coordination. Choose games that are appropriately rated for your child's age, which may include games rated *Early Childhood* or *Everyone*. Some games and apps will not be rated, but you are still likely to find parent-friendly reviews online. Try to utilize reviews provided by experts, because other parents may use their own values and opinions instead of objective measures and they can sometimes misjudge the appropriateness of content.

You may find using ebooks especially helpful at this age, because they offer an opportunity to practice reading skills. Continue to read with your child, especially if he enjoys it. Be aware that multimedia ebooks with music and movie clips could distract from the learning process and interfere with reading comprehension. On the other hand, some interactive elements can also help to keep kids engaged and interested. You need to participate in finding and discussing ebooks that best support your child's learning and interest in reading. You might find, for example, books that will read aloud to your child or help him sound out letters and words. These can obviously offer additional practice and further support learning. You can also contribute to your child's curiosity and interest in learning how things work with books that introduce basic knowledge about science, engineering or the arts. Choose any topic that interests your child and let him learn more. Showing your child that he can learn about new and interesting things in books is a great way to encourage reading.

There are many shows and movies that are appropriate for 5 and 6 year olds, but even more that are not. Your child does not yet have the viewing comprehension skills that are required to understand complex plots. This means that even if a story does not contain any inappropriate content, if it is not meant for his age group, he may not be able to fully enjoy and interpret the conclusion and theme. This becomes significant when subplots or even positive messages confuse younger children. Instead of absorbing examples of prosocial behavior, a child may easily understand and replicate bad behaviors that are demonstrated in a show because the consequences of these behaviors are too far removed from the action. Your child is also still working on distinguishing the worlds of fantasy and reality, so behavior that is "good" in a fantasy world, like Batman beating up an enemy, are not immediately understood as unacceptable in the real world. It is a safer bet to choose shows that are educational and/or made specifically for children this age. These shows are also more likely to support themes that are relevant to your child's current developmental goals, such as learning empathy. It is also still very necessary to avoid commercials and advertising in all shows. Your child is beginning to learn about and take on your family values. Commercials have the power to persuade all children, and despite your hard work, they will inevitably incite other kinds of thoughts and values, especially related to materialism.

Responsible Use Guidelines

As your child explores new kinds of games and shows, it may become even more important to supervise his media use. Your child may need some assistance to learn about these new media and games. He may also need help recognizing and responding to media that is not appropriate. Even with kid-friendly devices, good content guidelines and parental control options, it is very easy for your child to quickly and often unintentionally break the boundaries of content you find acceptable, or to accidentally make purchases or experience advertisement pop-ups. You need to help explain and manage content and options that are currently "above his pay grade". This will require you to be either regularly monitoring or directly supervising your child's use.

At this age you want to continue to instill the idea that media use is a privilege and that technology is to be respected. Help your child learn to use and store expensive devices with care and make sure that you model this in the way that you use your own devices. Time limits and content guidelines should be explicitly discussed with your child, so that he knows and understands the rules. You may want to use clocks and timers as references to help your child learn to set time boundaries and follow time limits, but you should still be in charge of helping your child stop and transition to new activities. As your child matures you may want to allow your child to start and stop his own timers or be responsible for turning off a show when it ends, but you still need to be available to help your child follow through. Total screen time should still be fairly limited. Children this age are not supposed to participate in sedentary activities for more than two hours at a time during the day. Try to keep total screen time to a maximum of two hours per day, and remember that this can add up quickly when apps and game time are included.

Activity Guidelines for 5 and 6 Year Olds

- At least 60 minutes of moderate to vigorous
- physical activity per day
- Physical activity should occur throughout the day in at least 15 minute increments
- Children need to experience a variety of physical activities
- Avoid extended periods of sedentary behavior (2 hours or more)

Media to Avoid

- Shows with stories meant for older children or adults
- Commercials and advergames
- Games that encourage violence and aggression
- Devices and games that involve or offer easy internet access (supervise all use on internet-based devices very closely)
- Internet messaging or texting services
- Social media (even if it claims to be kid-friendly)

Can violent media content increase aggressive behavior in your child?

Younger Children are especially prone to mimicking violent and aggressive behavior they view in media. They are pre-programmed to imitate what they see in order to integrate new information and behaviors into their understanding of the world. Even supposedly kid-friendly entertainment often contains frequent violence and

sometimes justifies aggressive behavior as socially acceptable. This is most obvious with superhero shows and characters. The effects of violent media content are mostly short-term, but children can become desensitized over time if they are repeatedly exposed to violent media content.
See the *Media Content Guidelines* chart for more information.

What about media that is introduced outside of our home?

Your child is old enough to begin really learning about and understanding rules. If you have regular discussions with your child about your family media guidelines and their purposes, he can become an important advocate in supporting them. Your child will likely experience some media and media content that you do not approve of, whether it's at school, a friend's house or even with other relatives or caretakers. If you have a policy of discussing your child's media use with him, he is more likely to talk with you about these experiences. You may want to use these opportunities as teaching moments to discuss any inappropriate content, ask your child questions, clarify any misinformation or misunderstanding and reinforce your family guidelines.

It is normal for children this age to explore the boundaries of rules or limits and to experiment with lying, but they can also be strong supporters of family rules especially if open communication is encouraged. You want to make your child feel safe to discuss other media experiences by demonstrating that you value honesty and that you want him to be able to talk to you. It is also helpful to understand that lying or breaking rules is normal at this age and just a part of another important learning process. You still want to enforce appropriate consequences for rule-breaking, but only if your child is responsible. In many cases, other adults or voices of authority may be responsible for breaking the rules. If this is the case and your child shared this information, applaud your child for recognizing that something wasn't right and having the courage to talk with you about it.

One way to demonstrate to your child that your family media guidelines are important is to talk about them openly with other parents, teachers and even relatives. There are ways to do this without being confrontational. Media guidelines are meant to be individualized to each family and child's needs, so the fact that your child may have different rules does not need to suggest anything about another family's rules. It is often easier to discuss this up-front just as you might mention any other special needs, phone numbers or regular business related to your child. You can also use some of the handouts included at the end of this workbook to help provide simple explanations of your expectations. If your child sees that you are an advocate for these guidelines outside of your home, this will only further instill their importance.

Tips for Discussing Inappropriate Media Content with your child

- Let your child know that you want to be able to talk with him about things that he sees in shows, games or on the internet and let him know that it is always okay to ask questions about things that he does not understand or that make him uncomfortable.
- Ask your child what feelings he had when he

113

experienced this content
- Explain to your child why this content is meant for adults or older children
- Provide as much information and facts about what he saw as you feel comfortable sharing
- Ask your child if he has questions about what he saw, and let him know that he can also ask questions later
- Make sure that your child understands that he is not bad because he saw these things, even if it was because he broke a rule about media use

Age 5-6 Guidelines	
New Media	Ebooks Games or apps for kids Educational shows without commercials *Books and reading should be encouraged*
Time Limits	Maximum of 2 hours per day
Content Guidelines	Ebooks for early reading Apps/games that are educational or encourage creativity, movement or simple problem solving Games rated for Early Childhood or some (E) Everyone Educational shows with no commercials Avoid frightening content Avoid violence and aggression without clear

	and immediate consequences
	Avoid media that includes stereotypes and gender bias
Responsible Use	Technology should be a privilege
	Expensive devices should be used and stored with care
	Discuss time limits and use verbal warnings to help prepare for transition
	Use clocks and timers for reference
	All content and use should be monitored

Chapter Summary
- Make time for activities that encourage reading skills
- Choose games and shows that are created for young children
- Try to keep media time educational
- Keep screen time to two hours a day or less
- Discuss media content with your child, especially if he is exposed to something unexpected or inappropriate

Creating personalized Guidelines for your 5 and 6 Year-Old
What new media will you introduce to your child?

When will you introduce it?

How will you incorporate media use into your child's routine?

How will you set and enforce limits for screen time?

Are there days when you will include less screen time for your child?

Are there days when you will include more screen time?

How will you reduce the potential for exposure to inappropriate content?

Who will discuss any inappropriate content that your child does experience with him or her?

How will you and other family members demonstrate responsible media use for your child?

If you have an older or younger child, how will you make adjustments for their different needs? (see Chapter 10 for ideas)

Ch. 8
7-8 Integrated Use: The Beginning

"In times of change, learners inherit the earth, while the learned find themselves beautifully equipped to deal with a world that no longer exists."
-Eric Hoffer

Developmental Priorities
- Develop more independence from parents and family
- Develop more awareness of others, the world and the future
- Increasing physical strength, stamina and coordination
- Become confident readers and writers

- Develop a strong sense of right and wrong and compassion for others
- Developing problem solving skills and understanding of consequences

At age seven your child is ready to begin really diving into new media. She now has the reasoning skills to analyze content, which opens up possibilities for exposure to new media platforms and more entertainment-based content. This is an excellent time to begin introducing important media literacy concepts to teach her about advertising and responsible use. As she learns to understand and use these new concepts and skills, you should discuss media content, to emphasize your family values, and provide knowledge to correct any misinformation. Your child will not learn to analyze the content she experiences unless you help her peak behind the curtain to see how media creators are trying to influence her. She will need help learning to be a critical viewer. These are important first steps which also help her learn to make good decisions when she begins creating her own content.

New Media and Technology

The first thing to begin introducing at this stage is basic media literacy concepts, especially about advertising. Your child has likely already learned to use many different kinds of devices and technology, but before she becomes a competent user she will need to fully understand new media's potential. She needs to learn that media can affect our behavior, perceptions and beliefs about different topics and the world. Early media literacy lessons should focus on advertising strategies and the impact and influence of mass media. They should also explain how and why media content is produced. Make sure you utilize resources, lessons and examples that are age-appropriate. Your child may learn some of this at school, but you should also become knowledgeable about these topics so you can emphasize them at home. True mastery of these concepts will require practice and discussion about the content to which she is exposed. Once she has a good understanding of the way that media can affect her, your child will be ready to begin thinking and learning about how the media that she creates can affect others. This will be especially important as she gets older and begins using new media to message and communicate with her friends.

With her new knowledge and skills your child will be ready to interact with media that is more focused on entertainment. She may be ready to play a wider variety of computer, video games and apps. She will also be interested in and ready to watch shows that are made for a general audience. All media content still needs to be monitored to make sure it is age-appropriate and commercials and advertising are kept to a minimum. It may become harder to find quality educational media that your child is interested in, but you can offer it when available. Children who watch more educational shows have been found to be more successful academically, especially compared to children who watch a lot of entertainment-based television. You may also decide to allow your child to begin using the internet, but only with you, under your direct guidance and supervision. You should use this as an opportunity to teach your child the basics of internet browsing and safety. When used appropriately, the internet can be a great way for you to stimulate and encourage your child's curiosity by helping her find information about the things that she is interested in.

Resources for Media Literacy Lessons
Media Smarts www.mediasmarts.ca
PBS Kids - "Don't Buy It" http://pbskids.org/dontbuyit/index.html
Long Live Kids - Media Literacy Lessons http://longlivekids.ca/media-literacy

Responsible Use Guidelines

As she becomes even more involved in a media-centric world it is very important that your child learns to respect you as her media ally and mentor. You want to create guidelines and rules that allow you to choose and discuss the games and shows that your child will use. Media use should still be a privilege that your child can earn by following your family rules and guidelines. Part of earning the opportunity to try new games and watch new shows might involve discussing choices with a parent. You want to do your best to make sure that your child knows you are available to discuss any uncomfortable or inappropriate content that she experiences. You can do this by clarifying for yourself and to your child that it is normal to make mistakes and stumble upon some bad content. This will likely be a learning process for you and your child because she will be interested in content that you might not have heard of or have any interest in. You can demonstrate the importance of being smart about media choices by taking the time to learn about the games and shows that your child is interested in.

Time limits for media use, especially screen media, are still important. Your child may engage with multiple media devices, which increases her overall exposure. It's important that she has plenty of downtime every day that does not involve screens or new media. Be sure to talk with your child about the importance of this downtime to allow her mind to rest and be creative in other ways. Your child is old enough to be learning about why you have guidelines for both media content and time limits. Explaining your reasons for family guidelines will help instill values related to living a more balanced life. Keep screen media exposure to one to two hours a day, especially for entertainment media. Your child may spend more time with technology as she gets older and uses it for school and social communication. You can begin allowing her to set her own timers or to turn of shows when they are over to help her begin self-monitoring her use, but you should still expect to supervise this process and help her follow through.

Media to Avoid
- Unsupervised internet use
- Games and apps that involve connection to an online community of players
- Games and shows that involve a lot of violence or complex plots
- Games that glorify violence or aggression
- Sexual content

- Apps, Games and shows that involve excessive advertising
- Unmediated news content
- Social Media (even if it claims to be kid-friendly)

What about media introduced outside of our home?

Your child will more than likely be introduced to new media outside of your home. Whether it's at school, a friend or relative's home, or even in your home under someone else's supervision, your child will likely experience media or media content that you did not expect. This may be frustrating at times, but it can also become an important learning experience for you and your child. Part of living in our modern digital world involves constantly being exposed to mass media and advertising. Even as adults we are generally exposed to more messages, prompts and advertising than we would prefer. You have probably experienced first-hand how easily you can stumble upon content that is offensive or makes you uncomfortable. Part of your child's journey towards media literacy and mastery will involve learning to manage invasive media. You can think of these early "oops experiences" as a beginner step in learning to navigate the unexpected. Right now your child is primarily a passive receiver of the media that is provided or allowed into her environment. However, you do want her to learn that she can make choices about what kind of content and how much media she is exposed to, so that as an adult she feels empowered to create a media balance that feels healthy. Even though you are still primarily responsible for making her media choices, you can begin to teach her about this process by discussing your choices and family media guidelines with her.

Here are three steps you can take to proactively manage outside media influence:
1) Help your child develop ownership of your family media guidelines
2) Communicate your guidelines to others
3) Plan for the unexpected and keep an open dialogue

Your child will feel more ownership over your family media guidelines if they are something that you regularly discuss and emphasize. Have conversations with her about why you chose certain rules or include or exclude certain media. This will allow her to feel more involved, to begin to understand the importance of your guidelines and to therefore value them. Children generally know if media is appropriate or inappropriate for them and will often identify this when asked. Your child may not necessarily do or say anything when she is presented with media choices outside of your guidelines, but she may be more likely to talk with you about her experience afterwards. If she believes that your family guidelines are important she is certainly more likely to make different choices when given the opportunity.

You can also be proactive about protecting your child from unwanted media experiences by communicating your family guidelines to others, especially teachers, other parents and relatives. If your child hears you providing this information to others, it will only emphasize in her mind the importance of these guidelines. Even with proactive discussion and planning, you should still expect these experiences to happen. The best way to plan for this is to talk with your child about how she may be exposed to things outside of your home that are not within your family guidelines. Help her to understand that while you do want to avoid this, it is important for her to talk to you about it when this happens. When it does happen, have a conversation with her about it. There may be content or information that she encountered that you want to discuss or clarify with her. Also, if you find that she spent too much time involved with media, you may want to ease off for a little while at home. Her experience may have also made her uncomfortable and it might be important for her to share her feelings about it with you.

Age 7-8 Guidelines	
New Media	Ebooks
	Games or apps with appropriate age ratings
	Shows for entertainment and education
	Fully supervised or assisted internet use
Time Limits	1-2 hours per day
Content Guidelines	Ebooks for young readers
	Games rated (E) for Everyone
	Avoid advertisements and commercials
	Avoid violence and aggression without clear and immediate consequences

	Avoid stories with plots that are overly complex
	Avoid excessive or graphic violence and violence without obvious consequences
Responsible Use	Technology should be a privilege
	Expensive devices should be used and stored with care
	Discuss time limits in advance
	Use clocks and timers for reference
	Expect to provide reminders and enforce time limits

Chapter Summary
- Discuss media content and messages with your child on a regular basis
- Teach your child about advertising and how media is used to influence people
- Encourage responsible use by discussing rules and time limits with your child and enforcing them
- Talk to your child about media she experiences outside of your home

Creating personalized Guidelines for your 7 and 8 Year-Old

What kind of new games, apps and shows will you let your child explore?

When will you introduce them?

What resources will you use to teach your child about how media influences people?

When will you discuss media content with your child?

How will you let your child get involved in keeping track of her media use?

When will you begin teaching your child about using the internet?

How will you encourage media content that is educational or may have educational benefits?

What will be your child's consequences for not following your family media guidelines?

How will you and other family members demonstrate responsible media use for your child?

If you have an older or younger child, how will you make adjustments for their different needs? (see Chapter 10 for ideas)

PART III: YOUR CHILD

Ch. 9

Special Situations: ADHD, Autism Spectrum Disorders, Anxiety/Depression, Early Trauma and "At-risk" youth populations

"Always be a first rate version of yourself and not a second rate version of someone else."
-Judy Garland

This chapter offers specific recommendations for children who have been diagnosed with ADHD, Autism Spectrum Disorder, Anxiety, Depression or who have experienced early childhood trauma or may be considered "at risk youth. All children are unique in their strengths and challenges and may require some modifications to the general guidelines offered in this book. Children with these issues in particular will certainly have different needs. Fortunately, new research findings allow us to make specific recommendations for children with these special situations. Some of these recommendations may be helpful even if your child only has some minor challenges related to his/her attention, focus, social skills, planning or executive functioning, anxiety or emotional resilience.

ADHD

Exhausted parents may find the time their children spend in front of the screen a welcome respite from the work of constantly redirecting their distracted child. However, children with ADHD have distinct challenges with media use. While each child's symptomology and challenges may differ, research shows that there are some common challenges related to media for children with ADHD. Digital media appears to affect these children differently and they also have significant risk factors for developing patterns of inappropriate use. Children with ADHD require additional guidance to develop media mastery and may need stricter media guidelines.

Self-control is one of the most significant factors related to a person's ability to appropriately manage media use, avoid overuse, distraction and addiction.[xxxviii] Children with ADHD have difficulty with self-control and therefore have difficulty learning to appropriately manage their media use. These children require more intervention and monitoring. Studies consistently show they are more vulnerable to video game addiction compared to their peers even when they play for the same quantity of time, and have more difficulty stopping.[xxxix] Risk factors for pathological gaming include low social competence and high impulsivity which are common symptoms of ADHD.

Pathological gaming is associated with depression, anxiety, social phobias, and lower school performance.[xl] Children with ADHD are also more vulnerable to internet addiction[xli] and more likely to enjoy television and to prefer it over non-media related entertainment such as reading.[xlii] Frequent television viewing in teenagers has been linked to increased attention difficulties, boredom and poor attitudes about school as well as poor academic performance including failure to complete homework, failure in high school and failure to attend college.[xliii] This is especially significant for children with ADHD who already struggle in these areas.

Use and especially overuse of media may also exacerbate symptoms or further impair the functioning of children with ADHD. Information overload, which occurs from overuse, makes appropriate processing of information and stimuli more difficult, exhausts mental resources, and may encourage habits of moving from one thing to the next.[xliv] Children with ADHD need to work harder than most to develop the ability to stay focused on one activity, so information overload definitely should be avoided. Gaming appears to exacerbate ADHD symptoms, though it is not known whether this is due to gaming itself, displacement of other important activities or potentially both.[xlv] Research shows that video game use negatively impacts attention span for children with ADHD.[xlvi] While certain types of video game play have been shown to improve attention in some children, this is not the case for children with ADHD.[xlvii] Because of its significant impact, computer and video game use should be limited to one hour per day for children with ADHD.[xlviii]

Recommendations:
- Limit screen time
- Plan screen time after important activities like homework
- Increase physical activity and outdoor time to counteract screen time
- Utilize co-viewing and discussion to increase video comprehension, especially social comprehension of media content
- Utilize rules and limits as a primary means to influence media use
- Avoid the use of guilt or shaming to attempt to modify behaviors because this can actually have the opposite effect[xlix]
- Encourage educational and slower-paced media activities and decrease time with fast-paced games and shows, which have been shown to temporarily impair some executive functioning[l]

Autism Spectrum Disorders

Most children with an Autism Spectrum Disorder (ASD) quickly become fascinated with digital media. Many will become preoccupied with specific video games or characters and may pursue these activities above most others. Parents may find that games or other media use is a good incentive to motivate other behaviors or as a helpful diversion during difficult situations. While many parents and professionals are supportive of the potential benefits and use of screen media and video games in particular, there are still some important considerations for creating individualized media guidelines.

Children with ASD still need to have their screen-media time limited to avoid potential health concerns and to make sure their development is not further disrupted by displacement of other important activities and social time. Research shows that children with ASD do spend more time with screen-media and they are also more likely to demonstrate problematic video game use.[li] Surveys show that media use is a preferred play activity for most children with ASD and most of these children exceed recommended screen time limitations.[lii] Further complicating the matter is the fact that children with ASD spend less time with socially interactive video games and social media and more time in solitary play.[liii] This means that these children are not benefiting from any of the potential social interaction often involved in modern gaming. This is unfortunate because these games could promote important social skills.

While more research is still needed, there are some studies that have demonstrated significant relationships between children with ASD and media use. For instance, screen-based media use has been shown to contribute to significant sleep problems in children with autism, especially when devices are located in the bedroom.[liv] This is a major concern because many children with ASD already experience problems with sleep disturbance. Excessive use and specific video games, especially role-playing and first-person shooter games, have also been shown to increase oppositional defiant behaviors in children with autism.[lv] While these challenges need to be taken into consideration when creating specialized guidelines, potential benefits should also be considered. Video games have been successfully used as a medium for encouraging social interaction and teaching social skills.[lvi] For some they can also be an important source for improving self-esteem because they offer the opportunity for improvement and mastery.[lvii]

Because of their appeal, new apps and screen-media devices are being created to aid in the development and mastery of communication skills in children with ASD. These devices show promise because they provide visual aids to help translate the communication process within a more comfortable medium, but more research is needed to establish their efficacy and to examine any potential trade-offs or harm. Concerns include the increase in screen-time and potential detriment to other important social skills and behaviors which may be compromised when a child spends most of his time looking at a screen. Media guidelines for children with ASD need to be much more individualized to accommodate the potential benefits and concerns related to each child's development. However, the same guidelines for daily screen-time limits should still be utilized at least for entertainment media.

Recommendations:
- Remove screen media from the bedroom and avoid frequent play right before bedtime
- Utilize screen time limitations to avoid overuse
- Encourage more educational games and avoid role-playing action games and first-person shooter games
- Take advantage of the attractiveness of digital media and use it to encourage social interaction through interactive video games, email and

messaging, and eventually other forms of social media

Anxiety & Depression

Children who have social anxiety or difficulty socializing may be attracted to media use and video games because they offer easy access to more instant gratification. This can be concerning if they develop habits of overuse because it detracts from important opportunities for social engagement. People who play video games excessively tend to have higher social anxiety and more trouble with interpersonal relationships.[lviii] Surveys suggest that many children use media as a way to cope with stress.[lix] Research also suggests that many young adults with depression and anxiety attempt to use media and the internet as a way to cope with their symptoms.[lx] This is generally not productive because it often leads to overuse which is shown to exacerbate symptoms. If your child struggles with anxiety or depression it is especially important to provide guidance related to their media use so that they do not develop long-term habits which may further impair their mental health.

Time limits for screen media are particularly important for children with anxiety and depression. Overuse can increase difficulty with sleep,[lxi] which is often already a challenge for these children. Sleep deprivation contributes to poor mental health. Children who spend more time with media are more likely to lack healthy habits such as going to bed on time and eating breakfast and they also report poorer health, more pain, illness and depression.[lxii] Excessive TV and computer use is linked to increased feelings of loneliness and sadness.[lxiii] Overuse can also increase the body's stress response and further inhibit a child's ability to feel calm and comforted.[lxiv]

Closely monitoring media content is also especially important for children with anxiety and depression because of its potential impact. Children who spend more time online and on the computer are more likely to have problematic internet experiences including exposure to more inappropriate content. This has been linked to increased symptoms of depression and anxiety.[lxv] Watching violent content can also increase anxiety, especially if violence is unjustified or unpunished.[lxvi] Exposure to TV newscasts has been associated with an increase in negative emotions.[lxvii] Research shows that kids who spend more time watching television are more likely to think that they are personally vulnerable to dangers in the world. This perception of vulnerability is actually greater for children with high anxiety levels.[lxviii] Short relaxation techniques, such as progressive relaxation, have been shown to help reduce the effects of exposure to upsetting media.[lxix]

There is also evidence that children with anxiety or depression tend to use media differently. Children with depression may be more likely to engage in unhealthy internet use.[lxx] Some children with poor social skills and low self-esteem are more likely to lie about themselves through media communication.[lxxi] This behavior does not contribute to the development of social skills and self-esteem and it can contribute to a reduced sense of wellbeing and poor mental health. With encouragement and guidance these children may be able to use media in ways that can improve their sense of wellbeing.

Researchers have shown that increasing computer use with friends is related to improved peer relationships in teenagers who are socially anxious.[lxxii] Socializing with friends through media use has been shown to make teens with depression and anxiety feel more socially supported, whereas surfing the internet can increase depression and anxiety.[lxxiii]

Recommendations:
- Set screen media time limits
- Avoid exposure to the news, especially when potentially disturbing content is present
- Monitor media content carefully to make sure it is age-appropriate and promotes healthy behaviors
- Utilize relaxation techniques to help mitigate the effects of upsetting media exposure
- Encourage these children to use media in more social ways, such as with friends or to communicate with friends, instead of spending time in more solitary activities

Early Trauma and "At-risk" Youth

The term "at-risk" has been used to mean different things in different contexts. For our purposes "at-risk" youth describes children who come from families and communities with fewer resources, children who experience family instability or dysfunction and racial or other discrimination. Each of these factors and especially a combination of these factors have been associated with a reduced chance for a child to successfully transition into a self-sufficient adulthood. In many cases these children's development will be significantly impacted by their early experiences and they lack some of the skills and resiliency of other children. Because of this they are more vulnerable to some of the potential harm related to media use, especially inappropriate media use. These children are also less likely, in many cases, to receive appropriate guidance and monitoring related to their media use. Children with specific early trauma experiences are also likely to have some of the same vulnerabilities and developmental considerations which place them "at-risk".

One of the greatest concerns for at-risk children is exposure to violence in media. Children who witness violence in person and on television are more likely to think that violence is normal and to be aggressive with others.[lxxiv] We know that brief exposure to violent video games increases aggressive behavior compared to nonviolent games, but highly aggressive children seem to be more strongly influenced by violent media exposure.[lxxv] Some "at risk" children, including those who struggle with aggression, are also more likely to be influenced by violent media and to actually engage in aggressive or violent behavior.[lxxvi] Early parental guidance, a healthy parental attachment bond, and strong emotional connection to adults and peers are the greatest protective factors for children's exposure to violent media. These are things that are often compromised for "at-risk" youth. Any child that has had early childhood experiences that make him more vulnerable should be exposed to less media violence.

"At-risk" children and families require more intervention to help reduce exposure to screen media. Children from low-income families with lower parent education experience more television exposure in early childhood and are at a greater risk for bullying involvement in elementary school.[lxxvii] Many "at-risk" children do not have the same quality early childcare experiences as other children. Preschoolers who are cared for in child care centers are exposed to less screen time. Children who are cared for primarily at home, in Head Start or in a home-based daycare spend much more time watching screens.[lxxviii] Other studies have shown that infants from low socioeconomic households experience more limited parent-child verbal interactions when their parents watch TV.[lxxix] This is deeply concerning because parent-child verbal interaction is critical for children to develop their communication skills. There may be a variety of reasons that vulnerable children are exposed to more daily screen time, but some are related to their home environment. Children whose mothers consider their neighborhood to be unsafe spend more time indoors and more time watching screen media.[lxxx] Children who live in high-crime neighborhoods with fewer recreational facilities also spend more time watching TV.[lxxxi]

Vulnerable or "at-risk" children are also likely to have emotional and behavioral problems, poor social skills, and attention problems which may require the same special considerations as those listed above for ADHD and anxiety or depression. It is important to consider that these children may have some developmental delays or learning challenges in a few or many areas. All age guidelines listed in this workbook are meant for children who fall within the normal or average range of development for their age. These may need to be modified to fit the "at risk" child's actual social, emotional, physical and cognitive development progress.

Recommendations:
- Set daily screen media time limits
- Monitor media content carefully to make sure it is age-appropriate and promotes healthy behaviors
- Avoid exposure to the news, especially when potentially disturbing content is present
- Actively avoid violent content in entertainment media and games
- Plan screen time after important activities like homework
- Increase physical activity and outdoor time to counteract screen time
- Utilize co-viewing and discussion to increase video comprehension, especially social comprehension of media content
- Remove screen media from the bedroom and avoid frequent play right before bedtime
- Viewing age-appropriate narrative programs has been shown to improve narrative skills in very young children who are at-risk.[lxxxii] This could be especially advantageous for children who are at risk academically.

Ch. 10
More Than One Child

"May your choices reflect your hopes, not your fears."
-Nelson Mandela

Parenting two or more children is definitely more than double the trouble, especially when each child has very different needs. This can make creating a family media plan seem like a lot of work. While there are additional challenges with multiple children, all family media guidelines are better if they incorporate the whole family and address differing needs, even if there is only one child. When parents and other family members are included in the plan they are able to model appropriate self-monitoring and to participate fully in the responsible use that promotes the health and wellbeing of each family member and the family as a whole. You may even find that children who are actively engaged in family media discussions learn to help out and teach each other as well. Multi-child family media guidelines do not have to be double or triple the amount of work.

Emphasizing diversity in your family can be a good way to approach the creation of family media guidelines for multiple children. This includes acknowledging that everyone is different and has their own strengths, weaknesses and personality. This can be more helpful than focusing on a child's age, because what's appropriate for one child at age seven may be something that your next child is not ready for at exactly the same age. It is also helpful for children to learn about their own strengths and weaknesses and to try not to compare themselves to others. This is a challenge when children are younger and are first learning about rules because they are interested in things being "fair". The 'fairness' phase is a developmentally appropriate attitude and is often part of the "tattling" phase that most kids go through. Having shared rules and individual rules can help. If you are consistent and upfront about consequences this also helps kids learn that rules are fair and predictable. When you plan your family media guidelines carefully you can feel confident that they are "fair" in the bigger picture because they support each person's growth and needs.

A Note on Being Fair

In parenting sometimes being fair is not about everybody being the same. Parents should consider the bigger picture of what will support the growth and wellbeing of each individual, which is unlikely to be exactly the same for each

---

child. It is the responsibility of parents to determine this and not a burden that children should take on, even when they want to try to understand. It might not be possible for children to fully understand their own needs or the needs of their siblings.

In many situations being fair is more often about equal amounts of love and attention. It doesn't mean measuring every moment of every day to be equal and exactly the same for each child. Every child has different needs for attention and care including the kind of affection and care they prefer. When differences become obvious, it is a good opportunity to talk about individual differences and needs. Talk about how everyone has different needs at different times and how in families everyone pitches in to help each other out as needed. When times are tough you may find that when one child has many needs, your other children begin acting out to get attention. This can be frustrating, but take it as a sign that your child does actually need more affection and care. Talk about the fact that he or she is wanting more from you, discuss better ways to ask for what they want, and plan something special. There should be consequences for acting out behavior, but you shouldn't punish your children for asking their family to meet their needs. Your children will learn how to balance relationships and individual needs from experiencing your leadership and skill in caring for your family. No parent can always balance this perfectly, but your children can learn much from how you handle and correct things.

Tips for Creating a Multi-Child Family Media Plan

- **Start with general rules for all family members:** These should be simple and promote the goals and values present in your family media plan (see sample plan for ideas)

- **Create specific guidelines for each child which include individual privileges and limitations**
- **Include guidelines that you create for yourself and other adults in the family in order to model responsible behavior and limit setting for your children**
- **Establish common consequences for breaking rules when possible:** An example would be losing a media privilege for a day. One child might end up losing TV time for a mistake and another might lose game time, but the consequence is still consistent for both.
- **Include family discussion, especially when guidelines are established or modified:** This way everyone knows all the rules and can learn from talking about them. This may encourage older children to participate in teaching younger children, which can enhance learning and adherence in both children.
- **Limit choices for your children both during the creation of guidelines and on a daily basis:** Giving children too many options requires a lot of energy and executive functioning and can be too much responsibility, even when it is meant as a privilege. Younger children should be given fewer options. Choices can increase with age and maturity. It can be especially helpful to avoid giving many choices at the end of the day or when your child is tired.

- **Plan time for separate activities for each child:** For example one has TV time, while the other one gets help with homework or plays outside. This may require additional planning, but it can also help you manage time and balance all your children's needs.
- **Plan ahead, but also have fail safe activities you can fall back on:** You won't need to use entertainment media as a babysitter as much if you plan ahead. It may seem like making all these plans ahead of time will require a lot of energy and work, but it will be completely worth it. Advanced planning reduces the energy required for managing the chaos, and behavior challenges associated with a lack of structure. One way to help yourself out is to create and stick to a routine and have some fail safe activities for the unexpected or situations when you just can't plan ahead. Examples of fail safe activities can include special games, activities or treats that you only allow or provide at certain times. This could be a book that the family reads aloud together or special coloring books, activity sets that are completed individually or a night out for pizza. You might also want to keep some media options that are enjoyable and appropriate for all family members. If you have some backup plans that are not media-centered you may have an easier time managing your children's screen time.
- **Plan time to rethink your plans and guidelines for each family member:** As your children mature and new technology

emerges you will need to modify your guidelines. Expect to make many changes and updates, both planned and unplanned. Before birthdays, the end of the school year or the upcoming completion of major accomplishments or activities are good times to reevaluate and make plans for your next discussion. Being proactive about planning can make the consistent need for changes seem less overwhelming.

SAMPLE FAMILY MEDIA PLAN

Family Rules:
> **Digital devices are treated with respect**
> **Media Time is a privilege**

In your home this might mean time together, homework, outdoor/exercise, and chores take priority.
> **People and family time come first**

This concept can be used to settle disputes and implement strategies with a person-centered caring approach that teaches relationship skills. Ex. older child wants to watch a show that younger child cannot watch, so according to the family rule the priority in navigating this discussion is to maintain good relationships. If children fight
about media time and have difficulty even with parental intervention, then media time privileges are taken away. This promotes the importance of being respectful of others despite individual desires.
> **All family members talk with a parent when they**
> **experience things in shows, movies, games or**
> **online that are new or upsetting**

Let kids know that this means that parents also talk with each other or other adults about some things they see or hear about, because this sets a good example.

146

Individual Guidelines:

Child 1:

- Can watch parent-approved* TV shows on video or approved apps as long as she is following the family rules
  o One show or 20 minutes of game time allowed on weeknights when there is time
  o Up to three shows on a weekend day or 30 minutes of game time

-Consequence for breaking a rule or guidelines is losing a day of media privilege

Child 2:

- Can watch parent-approved TV shows on video with Child 1 or
- Can watch other parent-approved* shows or movies when Child 1 is not present as long as he is following the family rules
  o One show or 20 minutes of game time allowed on weeknights when there is time
  o Up to three shows or one movie or one hour of game time on a weekend day
  o Can use the computer to get online with a parent or at school

-Consequence for breaking a rule or guidelines is losing a day of media privilege

Parent 1:

- Can watch shows with kids or
- Can watch adult content when kids are asleep or not home
- Will not use cell phone (including talking, texting, apps, email) at dinner or during family time unless it's a special situation

Parent 2:

- • Can watch shows with kids or
- • Can watch adult content when kids are asleep or not home
- o Will not use cell phone (including talking, texting, apps, email) at dinner or during family time unless it's a special situation
- o Will not check work emails on the weekend unless it's a special situation

All family rules and examples of how they apply should be discussed as a family. This might mean having multiple discussions. Individual guidelines could be discussed as a group and also individually depending on what feels most appropriate for your family.

*It might be helpful to keep a list of currently approved shows or apps to help communication between parents or other caregivers

Ch. 11
Tips for Instituting Guidelines: It's Never Too Late

"If nothing ever changed there would be no butterflies"
-Author unknown

Instituting family media guidelines can be beneficial at any time regardless of your child's age or previous experience with media. You may have learned that your child is using media or being exposed to content that is not developmentally appropriate for him. Maybe you feel it is harsh or hypocritical to change his privileges all of a sudden. Don't let this stop you from implementing changes which can benefit your child and teach him valuable lessons about developing media mastery and responsible media consumption. Most parents have not been given appropriate information or solid guidelines for

149

supervising their children's media use because technology has been developing so rapidly. The important thing to remember is that your children can benefit from witnessing how you handle this transition. New technology, research and knowledge will influence many opportunities for change in their lifetime. It's important for your children to learn to adapt as new knowledge offers better options for supporting their health and wellbeing. You want them to learn to utilize new information to their benefit, even if it requires making some difficult changes. This might be your opportunity to set that example.

Implementing change in your family is likely to come with some challenges. Every individual reacts to change differently, so expect different things from each child and also from the adults in the family. It is important that parents take the lead in implementing changes and helping all family members to adapt. Expecting some push back and challenges can help you be mentally prepared, but try to stay positive. You should carefully choose a timeline and strategy for implementing changes that will set family members up for success. Don't put off making changes indefinitely, but it's okay to choose to do this when you have the time and energy to provide the additional support and supervision your family needs to get started. Include your children in discussions about family media guidelines. This is important for your success. It is also an opportunity for you to teach media literacy. Including your children will increase their sense of ownership over the family guidelines and will make them feel more comfortable talking with you about their media experiences. Remember that your children will learn how to manage change by participating in family transitions and watching how you handle them, including how you manage the inevitable missteps along the way. You may also learn some new things about your children and your own resilience. Humans are very adaptable and practicing flexibility and coping with change only increases our resilience.

Tips for Implementing Change

- **Consider planning ahead of time**. Example: Have a talk on Friday night and start the new plan for instituting family guidelines on Monday. Remember that different family members may need more time to adjust and mentally prepare for change.

- **Have a parent-to-parent conversation** about instituting new guidelines before having a family talk to make sure all parents and caregivers are on the same page and can be consistent

- **Have a family discussion** to allow all family members to participate in developing the guidelines so that each family member feels involved and can more easily develop ownership of the new rules. Making changes as a family can help create a supportive environment where everyone is involved in taking charge of their media use.

- **Talk about the process of change** as part of your family discussion and have family members identify things about the changes that they think might be easy or hard.

- **Write down your family plan, rules and guidelines** and use pictures if possible for younger children who can't read.
- **Include consequences** for breaking rules as part of the plan and discuss them as a family.
- **Plan for another family discussion** after implementing changes to discuss challenges and progress. This could be after a week, a month or whenever you think it would be helpful.
- Make sure you also **make time along the way to talk with family members** about challenges, both individually or as a family.
- **Discuss appropriate media and content guidelines with your children** on a regular basis. Many times your child will know and understand when something is not age-appropriate and they will be more likely to discuss this with you or others if you keep them involved in this type of communication.
- **Allow all family members to participate in discussion**, even though parents will make the ultimate decisions. Ask your older children if they think that something is appropriate for their younger sibling and have a family discussion about it. This can create a family culture of safety where everyone takes on some responsibility for looking out for each other and all members feel comfortable talking about their experiences.
- **Before implementing family media guidelines consider your own media use**

and think about whether or not there are changes
you want to implement for yourself.

- **Be a role model for change** and
discuss your own challenges with managing
media, when appropriate. An important part of
media literacy is learning how media influences
our thoughts, feelings and behaviors. When
children understand this and they witness parents
and other role models who modify their choices
and behaviors because of this, they learn to be
critical users.

- **Consider setting individual and
family goals** to get started and don't expect
perfection. Talk about how it might be hard to
learn a new way of doing things and about how
each family member can support each other.

- **Make plans for self-care** or set up a
support system to help you manage your own
stress and challenges related to implementing
these changes

Common Reactions or Behaviors to Expect

- Anger outbursts, frustration and irritability
- Excitement
- Sadness or Anxiety
- Curiosity
- Passivity or indifference
- Some children may shut down and have a hard
time participating in discussions at first
- Arguing or fighting between family members
- Regressive behaviors

- It may be helpful to assume that some family members will surprise you, both in positive and challenging ways

Remember: creating more structure ultimately reduces your children's anxiety and allows them to focus on and engage in other important developmental tasks

PART IV: CHARTS AND FORMS

List of Charts and Forms

Screen Time Charts

Track your family's screen time along with time spent exercising and engaging in rejuvenating relaxation activities to get an idea of your current balance. You can also use these to create weekly media plans which can be helpful when initiating changes. See the example charts below for some ideas.

3-4 Year Old Screen Time Chart

WEEK 1	Monday	Tuesday	Wednesday	Thursday	Friday	Saturday	Sunday
Screen Time							
Movie/Show							
Games							
Outside Play							
Free Play							
Reading							

WEEK 2	Monday	Tuesday	Wednesday	Thursday	Friday	Saturday	Sunday
Screen Time							
Movie/Show							
Games							
Outside Play							
Free Play							
Reading							

Example 3-4 Year Old Screen Time Chart (Week 1)

WEEK 1	Monday	Tuesday	Wednesday	Thursday	Friday	Saturday	Sunday
Screen Time							
Movie/Show	20 min.		NO SCREEN DAY		Movie Night 90 min.	20 min.	NO SCREEN DAY
Games		15 min.		15 min.			
Outside Play	60 min. + 60 min.	120 min.	120 min.	60 min.	30 min.	120 min.	120 min.
Free Play				60 min.			
Reading	15 min.	10 min.	15 min.	15 min.	15 min.		15 min.

Early Childhood Media Mastery: A Complete Guide to Teaching
Smart & Responsible Media Use

5-6 Year Old Screen Time Chart

	Monday	Tuesday	Wednesday	Thursday	Friday	Saturday	Sunday
Entertainment							
Computer/Video Games							
TV							
Movie							
Education							
Movie at School							
Games							
Total Screen Time							
Exercise							
Sports or Other Activity							
Outside Play							
Total Minutes							
Relaxation							
(Reading, Drawing/ Painting, Puzzles - cannot include screens!)							
Goal:							

Example 5-6 Year Old Screen Time Chart

	Monday	Tuesday	Wednesday	Thursday	Friday	Saturday	Sunday
Entertainment							
Computer/Video Games	Playstation 30 minutes	Playstation 30 minutes	Playstation 30 minutes	Playstation 30 minutes			Playstation 30 minutes
TV						Backyardigans 60 minutes	
Movie					Family Movie Night- 120 min.		
Education							
Movie at School							
Games	Knowledge Adventure- 30m		Knowledge Adventure- 30m				
Total Screen Time	60 min.	30 min.	60 min.	30 min.	130 min.	60 min.	30 min.
Exercise							
Sports or Other Activity		Baseball Practice		Baseball Practice		Trampoline Party	Baseball Game
Outside Play	Play Outside		Play Outside		Play Outside	Play Outside	
Total Minutes	60 min.	60 min.	60 min.	60 min.	60 min.	3 hours	60 min.
Relaxation (Reading, Drawing/Painting, Puzzles - cannot include screens!)	Bedtime Story	Bedtime Story	Bedtime Story	Bedtime Story	Bedtime Story	Board games	Painting Activity
Goal:	20 min./day						

7+ Screen Time Chart

	Monday	Tuesday	Wednesday	Thursday	Friday	Saturday	Sunday
Entertainment							
Computer/Video Games							
TV							
Movie							
Total Minutes							
Education							
Movie at School							
Computer Time							
Total Minutes							
Total Screen Time							
Exercise							
Sports or Other Activity							
Outside Play							
Total Minutes							
Relaxation							
(Reading, Drawing/ Painting, Puzzles - cannot include screens!)							
Goal:							

Example 7+ Screen Time Chart

	Monday	Tuesday	Wednesday	Thursday	Friday	Saturday	Sunday
Entertainment							
Computer/Video Games	30 min.	30 min.		30 min.		60 min.	30 min.
TV							
Movie					120 min.		
Total Minutes	30 min.	30 min.		30 min.	120 min.	60 min.	30 min.
Education							
Movie at School			120 min.				
Computer Time	30 min.	30 min.		30 min.			30 min.
Total Minutes	30 min.	30 min.	120 min.	30 min.			30 min.
Total Screen Time	60 min.	60 min.	120 min.	60 min.	120 min.	60 min.	60 min.
Exercise							
Sports or Other Activity		60 min.		60 min.			
Outside Play	60 min.		60 min.		30 min.	120 min.	120 min.
Total Minutes	60 min.	60 min.	60 min.	60 min.	30 min.	120 min.	120 min.
Relaxation (Reading, Drawing/Painting, Puzzles - cannot include screens!)	10 min.	30 min.	30 min.	30 min.		30 min.	60 min.
Goal:	30 min./day						

MEDIA USE HIERARCHY

Media	Age Range for Introduction	Explanation
Recorded Music	Birth	Music helps to soothe babies and to develop emotional regulation. Media devices can be used to provide a variety of recorded music, but make sure you stay in charge of digital devices until your child is old enough to use all of their functions appropriately.
Books	Birth (ebooks: 2-5) (Multimedia ebooks. 5+)	Babies can benefit from reading time from a very early age. Ebooks can be introduced around two or three with supervision, but are most beneficial if an adult is still reading them to your child. Multimedia ebooks/magazines and recorded books are too distracting and advanced for preschoolers.
Interactive Educational Games (apps, video/ computer games)	3-5	This can include creative games that involve painting drawing or making music, which are educational at this age because they allow

		children to develop some fine motor skills. It is important to note that drawing and writing with actual utensils is even more important and should not be replaced. Touchscreen apps are a great place to start because young children have the ability to pinch and touch well before they can click or type.
Educational Movies and Shows with no commercials	3-4	Educational cartoons attempt to incorporate an interactive quality by asking questions and encouraging children to respond. Other shows can introduce different cultures and explore topics related to science, art or history. Younger children still confuse fiction and reality, especially in live-action representations (anything not animated) and their screen time should be more limited so they can continue to develop skills through hands-on play. Also keep in mind that most children will struggle to follow many TV/Movie plots

		until they are 9 or 10. Just because they watch a show does not mean that they are following the story or understanding the intended messages.
Games and TV for entertainment (little or no educational value)	7-8	Other games and TV shows will become more accessible to this age group, but they should still contain age-appropriate content and promote positive values.
TV with commercials	7-9	Around age 7 children can begin to learn about advertising and the techniques used to "trick" people into thinking about and wanting products. Once your child has developed media literacy related to advertising, she can begin to think critically about commercials. Even with these tools, its better to avoid commercials when possible because they can still have a powerful effect on your child's thoughts and preferences.
Messaging (Email, texting, chats)	8-11	Early messaging experiences should be fully supervised by a

		parent and should not occur within a social media context which requires additional media literacy and maturity. Putting off texting and messaging may help your child to develop formal writing skills before they start using text lingo. Kids will eventually need to learn to move fluidly between different languages (text, casual, formal written English) as they navigate many different communication outlets. Parents and teachers can facilitate this by discussing the importance of context and by allowing children to become proficient at a language before they take on two more. It's okay for your child to let her friend know she will bbl (be back later), but you also want her to be able to spell it out when she needs to.
Internet Use	7 (supervised) 9-10 (monitored)	Children can begin to watch you navigate the internet at a young age, but should not be set free (even with supervision)

		until they are 9-10 and they have completed some basic media literacy training. Your child is not able to fully understand the concept of a global network and the way the internet functions until they are about 13 years old.
Social Media	12-15	Responsible social media use requires a complex understanding of the internet and it's potential which is not usually seen in children under the age of 13. Most social media sites also have a minimum age requirement of 13. Teen users will also need to have a fluent understanding of relevant media literacy concepts so they can make good decisions about the many complex social situations they may face when using this media.

Media Content Guidelines		
CONTENT	AGE	EXPLANATION
Cartoon Violence/ Unrealistic Violence	4+	Until the age of 4 or 5 children will often have difficulty making judgements about whether or not something represented on a screen is potentially real or not. This ability will further develop by the age of 6 or 7, when a child will be more able to determine if depictions are reasonable or possible.
Unpunished Violence/ Violence without Consequences Content or characters that exhibit antisocial or discriminatory behavior or reinforce stereotypes, including gender stereotypes	7+	Until most children are about 7 yrs. old they will likely focus on whether a character was punished for engaging in violent behavior in order to determine if the behavior is right or wrong. Older children are able to consider the character's reason for engaging in violence and are less likely to see violent characters as role models even if they are attractive characters or their behavior goes unpunished. At seven you can begin talking to your child about discriminatory behavior and stereotypes. As part of media literacy discussions you can talk about the ways that media

		can reinforce these ideas. You should still try to avoid content that does not promote the positive values that fit with your family's belief system.
Violence as part of complex plots (ie. revenge, delayed consequences or outcomes)	9+	Children younger than 9 or 10 are often unable to make inferences about plot and subplot connections and may not make connections if there is a time-delay in a story or a break, such as a commercial.
Sexual Content that discusses and promotes healthy attitudes about sex and relevant consequences	11+	Curiosity, exploration and humor related to sexuality are a normal part of life for middle school children. Parents can utilize themes and scenes from movies and TV to help discuss this topic and address questions and real-world concerns.
Intricate Movie Plots Complex Video Games with Violence Content with Alcohol, drug and tobacco use that demonstrates consequences of use	13+	Preteens and Teens are developing metacognitive thinking skills which will allow them to understand and adjust their own thought processes related to the content they experience in entertainment.

| Unmonitored exposure to entertainment violence and content with Alcohol, drug and tobacco use that does not demonstrate consequences of use or makes light of it | 17+ | All teens are subject to an adolescent egocentrism which means that while they may recognize a behavior as risky or dangerous, they are likely to underestimate their own personal risk due to feelings of invulnerability. There is some evidence that repeated exposure to entertainment violence in early adolescence can impair a teens ability to make good choices related to the use of weapons and physical aggression.[lxxxiii] |

RESPONSIBLE AND INDEPENDENT MEDIA USE HIERARCHY		
STAGE	AGE RANGE	INSTRUCTIONS
Routine and Redirection	0-4	Young children are especially likely to struggle with transitions from stimulating activities and they have little to no concept of time. The use of redirection (distracting attention to another activity) and using natural endings and conclusions can help with this. **Example of Redirection-** use music or songs to signal transition to the next activity or introduce a planned drink or snack to end media time **Examples of Natural Endings-** Set a game to end at 10 minutes (or device to turn off) or play a 20 minutes show and turn off right at the end. These proactive steps can save both you and your child a lot of energy and potential frustration.
Complete Parental Monitoring With Warnings	3-6	All media should be carefully chosen and monitored by parents. Explicitly discuss time limits and schedules with your child and provide warnings to prepare your child for transitions when appropriate. **Examples-** Provide 5 and 1

		minute time warnings; Set a timer and show your child how screen time will end when the timer beeps
Parental Monitoring & Assistance	6-12	School-aged children are ready to begin taking on some responsibility for their media use, but guidelines for media use should still be set by parents. Allow your child to set the timer and/or turn off devices themselves, but expect him/her to need continued reminders. Choices related to new games or shows and media content should be discussed, but decisions should ultimately be made by parents. **Example**- Download a game timer app and use it to help your child turn off the device after the allotted time. **Hint**- Routines are still important. Building entertainment time into your child's schedule can help set expectations and make it easier to stop and move on to the next activity.
Collaborative Planning and Decision Making	11-15	Allow pre-teens and teens to participate in discussing and creating their own limits and schedules for screen-time and digital media. Parents should

		still be involved in helping them make appropriate choices and regularly monitoring and discussing content, especially as social media becomes a part of their life.
Open-Ended Communication & Periodic Monitoring	14-18	Teenagers are more than ready to announce their independence and take control of their own habits and media use, but parents can still provide helpful guidance. By keeping up open-ended communication with your teen and being involved in his digital life, you can provide guidance and help him think critically about the choices he makes. Expect your teen to make some mistakes along the way, but use these opportunities to have a discussion so you can help him learn better ways to use media in the future.

Video Game Type Guidelines		
Game Type	**Age-Range for Introduction**	**Explanation**
Educational	2+	*Games that are specifically designed to teach new skills* **The educational goals and lessons in these games should be age-appropriate for your child. You should also take into account your child's developmental abilities and current skill set in order to choose appropriate games.** Examples: Sesame Street: Cookies Counting Carnival Sesame Street: Elmo's Musical Monsterpiece
Puzzle Games	6+	*Players solve puzzles or problems that can involve the exercise of logic, memory, pattern matching, and reaction time* **These games will require your child to**

		have puzzle-solving experience and mastery of basic problem solving skills. Many puzzle games will be too advanced for elementary school children, but there are some intended for younger players. Examples: Angry Birds Candy Crush Tetris*
Rhythm Games	5-7	*Require the player to undertake some action such as follow a sequence of movement, or develop specific rhythms in response to music or other stimuli* **Very young children do not yet have the skills required to participate in these games. These games can help develop coordination and motor skills, but the music content must be age-appropriate. Look for kid versions to introduce**

		to younger children. Examples: Just Dance Kids Dance Dance Revolution Guitar Hero*
Platform	6-7	*This genre often requires the protagonist to run and jump between surfaces (i.e. platforms) whilst avoiding game objects and the detrimental effects of gravity* **Many of these games are simple enough for younger children, but they usually do not have any educational value or require a lot of complex thinking.** Examples: Madagascar 3: The Video Game Super Mario 3D Land
Racing	6-8	*Typically place the player behind the wheel and involve competing in a race against other drivers*

		and/or time **These games rarely have any educational value and often involve or encourage aggression or violence.** Examples: Mario Kart Grand Prix Legends
Role Playing (RPG)	7	*Player assumes the role of a fictional character, usually in a fantasy setting* **These games can encourage imaginative play. Simple kid-friendly games are available for kids as young as 7 or 8.** Examples: Bee Movie Game Herotopia Planet Crashers
Sports	6-10	*Simulate the sporting experience; some place the emphasis on the experience of playing the sport, whilst others focus on the strategy behind the sport*

		Most sports games are not appropriate for the younger age-range, but there are a few made specifically for younger children. Look for games that require movement to allow for physical activity and development of coordination and gross motor skills. Example: Wii Sports
Action	7-8	*Typified by fast-paced events and movement which often have to be performed reflexively; Player often controls avatar of a protagonist* ☐ **These games may increase reaction speed and hand-eye coordination, but they are less likely to contain puzzles or challenges that require problem solving skills** Example: Frogger

Traditional	7-10	*Computerized versions of board, word, and card games* **Most board games are too advanced for early childhood. Young children will also benefit more from playing games with live individuals so that they can develop appropriate social skills and learn about good sportsmanship.** Examples: Chess Poker
Action-Adventure	8	*Involve both exploration and puzzle solving alongside fast-paced action sequences* □ **These games may involve more narrative and problem solving than simple action games. Look for games made for kids to make sure they are not too challenging and content is age-appropriate.**

		Example: Skylanders Lego: Harry Potter
Simulation	8-10	*Some aim to simulate physical activities such as flying an aircraft; Other forms of simulation games aim to provide simulations of forms of management, such as city management* **These games may involve complex strategies and advanced problem solving and planning skills. Many of these games will contain experiences and concepts that are not appropriate for children, so be sure to check content. Some simulation games that are appropriate for young children will fall under the educational category.** Examples: Sim Animals Madden NFL Farmville

Social Marketing Games	10+	*Games designed to promote specific causes, issues or behaviors ex. Smoking Prevention, Stay in School* **Despite their claims these games are not always created to be age-appropriate and often allow players to engage in the "bad behaviors" that the game is meant to prevent. Children will need strong media literacy skills and the ability to analyze the message they are receiving in order to understand and make their own decisions about these issues and behaviors. Learn more about these games before allowing your child to play.** *Also be aware of recruitment games on the internet, which are often sponsored by extremist organizations and*

		specifically target children. These games should always be avoided because they contain harmful propaganda. Example: Smoke Free Kids: Clear the Air
Adventure	10-13	*The player is the protagonist in an interactive story and in order to progress must solve puzzles* **These games usually contain a variety of puzzles and complex story lines that test memory and attention. They can develop deductive reasoning skills, logic and memory, but many contain mature content.** Examples: Back to the Future: The Game Broken Sword Sam & Max
Turn-Based Strategy	11-13	*A strategy game, usually related to warfare, where players take turns in*

		much the same way as with many traditional board games **Strategy-based video games have been shown to improve players' cognitive flexibility. Some of these games will be accessible at age 11, but most will be too challenging.** Examples: Civilization Endless Space Age of Wonders
First Person Shooter Games	12-13	*Action games where the player is "behind the eyes" of the game character in a first-person perspective; Some also support third-person views* □ **Some of these games will contain more narrative or puzzles. Games with milder violence may be acceptable for young teens.** Examples: GoldenEye 007 Star Fox: Assault
Fighting	13	*Player fights other*

		players or the computer in some form of one-on-one combat □ **These games are purely for entertainment and are violent by concept. Although the intensity of violence varies, these games are definitely not appropriate for younger children.** Examples: Playstation All-Stars Battle Royale* Street Fighter
Real-time Strategy (RTS)	13	*Typically define a number of goals around resource collection, base and unit construction and engagement in combat with other players or computer opponents who also share similar goals* **These complex strategy games may require micro & macro management skills to successfully manage both short-term and long-term**

		goals within the game. Examples: Age of Empire Clash of Clans StarCraft
Advergames	13+	*Includes anything produced commercially which promotes a product or brand* **These games are often free. They are intentionally manipulative and utilize the power of the immediate feedback/reward system inherent in games to create positive associations in the brain related to products or brands. They are potentially even more effective than traditional advertising, which can have a profound impact on children's behavior and choices. Even adults should use their knowledge about media and**

		advertising to make informed decisions about their exposure to these games. These games require a strong knowledge and understanding of media literacy in order to undermine their possible impact. Younger children do not have the ability to manage these games appropriately. Examples: America's Army Pepsi Invaders Taco Bell: Taco Fu
Massively Multiplayer Online Role Playing Games	13-15	*Multiplayer role-playing games that involve a persistent world where many players (usually worldwide) interact through the internet* □ **These games will involve the same caution/concerns related to participating in social media. The appropriate age to begin playing will**

		depend on the maturity of the child, content of games, and parent comfort with the potential exposure to adult content and interaction. Some supervision or discussion of game play is recommended for younger teens. Examples: World of Warcraft EverQuest II Guild Wars
Stealth	Most not suitable for children	*Games which can be defined by a focus on subterfuge and/ or precision play; Includes themes of espionage, counter-terrorism and rogue characters*
Survival Horror	Most not suitable for children	*Often an action-adventure or first-person shooter with a focus on fear and survival and adopting many of the elements of traditional horror fiction*

*Examples listed are examples of the game type and

are not necessarily appropriate games to introduce to beginners of that particular game genre

There is a possible cathartic effect related to playing violent games, but they can also increase aggression in the short term. They should be played in moderation and at times that won't interfere with subsequent activities (avoid bedtime or before school).

0-2 Year Old Guidelines	
*Do not introduce screen media into your child's daily routine until they are at least 2 years old	
Beneficial Media Experiences	Print media including baby books, picture books and reading time Music including digitally recorded music; Singing along and dancing with your child may have increased benefit (be sure to also encourage music making with simple instruments)
Experiences to Avoid	Avoid background television which can affect your child's attention and negatively impact important play and learning activities Keep digital devices such as smart phones out of reach of young children; When they are ready to use these you will want them to learn to treat them with respect and to use them appropriately, which may be difficult if they have already been introduced as toys Try to keep your own digital media use to a minimum when you are directly supervising or engaging with your child because this can negatively impact important bonding time and relationship feedback which affects your child's brain development

Age 3-4 Guidelines	
Beginner Media	Ebooks Simple Games or Apps Shows without commercials *Continue providing music and books*
Time Limits	1 hour per day of screen time (2 hours maximum) Aim for short time periods like a 20 minute show or 15 minutes of game time to reduce sedentary time
Content Guidelines	Simple ebooks with lots of pictures Apps/Games that mimic play (painting, drawing, building) Games rated for Early Childhood Interactive Early Childhood shows without commercials Look for educational content Avoid violence and scary scenes or characters Avoid media that includes stereotypes and gender bias
Responsible Use	Make technology a privilege Teach your child to be careful with expensive devices Use Routine and Redirection to help your child transition to different activities

Age 5-6 Guidelines	
New Media	Ebooks
	Games or apps for kids
	Educational shows without commercials
	Books and reading should be encouraged
Time Limits	Maximum of 2 hours per day
Content Guidelines	Ebooks for early reading
	Apps/games that are educational or encourage creativity, movement or simple problem solving
	Games rated for Early Childhood or some (E) Everyone
	Educational shows with no commercials
	Avoid frightening content
	Avoid violence and aggression without clear and immediate consequences
	Avoid media that includes stereotypes and gender bias
Responsible Use	Technology should be a privilege
	Expensive devices should be used and stored with care
	Discuss time limits and use verbal warnings to help prepare for transition
	Use clocks and timers for reference All content and use should be monitored

Age 7-8 Guidelines	
New Media	Ebooks
	Games or apps with appropriate age ratings
	Shows for entertainment and education
	Fully supervised or assisted internet use
Time Limits	1-2 hours per day
Content Guidelines	Ebooks for young readers
	Games rated (E) for Everyone
	Avoid advertisements and commercials
	Avoid violence and aggression without clear and immediate consequences
	Avoid stories with plots that are overly complex
	Avoid excessive or graphic violence and violence without obvious consequences
Responsible Use	Technology should be a privilege
	Expensive devices should be used and stored with care
	Discuss time limits in advance
	Use clocks and timers for reference
	Expect to provide reminders and enforce time limits

Caregiver Handout- Family Media Guidelines

In our family the **Family Media Use Rules** are:

Individual Guidelines Include:

Types of Media:

Daily Media Time Limits:

Parent Approved Shows and Games:

General Media Content Guidelines:

Other Notes:

Digital media experiences that family members enjoy together right now include:

[i] Siegel, D. (1999). *The developing mind: How relationships and the brain interact to shape who we are.* New York: Guilford Press.

[ii] Calvert, S., & Wilson, B.J. (2008). Attention and Learning from Media during Infancy and Early childhood. In *The handbook of children, media, and development.* Chichester, U.K.: Wiley-Blackwell.

[iii] Troseth, G.L. (2003). The medium can obscure the message: Young children's understanding of video. *Child Development,* 69, 950-65.

[iv] Calvert, S. (2008). Attention and Learning from Media during Infancy and Early childhood. In *The handbook of children, media, and development.* Chichester, U.K.: Wiley-Blackwell.

[v] Dworak, M., Schierl, T., Bruns, T., & Strüder, H. K. (2007). Impact of singular excessive computer game and television exposure on sleep patterns and memory performance of school-aged children, *Pediatrics,* 120(5), 978-85

[vi] Kalnin, A. J., Wang, Y., Kronenberg, W. G., Mosier, K. M., Hummer, T. A., Dunn, D. W., Matthews, V. P. (2010). Short-term violent video game play by adolescents alters prefrontal activity during cognitive inhibition, *Media Psychology,* 13(2), 136-154

[vii] Bartlett, C. P., Rodeheffer, C. (2009). Effects of realism on extended violent and nonviolent video game play on aggressive thoughts, feelings, and physiological arousal, *Aggressive Behavior,* 35(3), 213-224

[viii] Christine Rosen, "The Myth of Multitasking, " *The New Atlantis*, Spring 2008, www.thenewatlantis.com

[ix] *Hart, A. (2013). The digital invasion: How technology is shaping you and your relationships. Grand Rapids, MI: Baker Books., 65.*

[x] Wilson, B.J. (2011) *Media Violence and Aggression in Youth* In The Handbook of Children, Media and Development edited by Calvert, S.J. & Wilson, B.J.

[xi] Meaney, M. J. (2001). Maternal care, gene expression, and the transmission of individual differences in stress reactivity across generations. *Annual Review of Neuroscience*, 24(1), 1161-1192

[xii] David Gerry, Andrea Unrau, Laurel J. Trainor. Active music classes in infancy enhance musical, communicative and social development. *Developmental Science*, 2012; 15 (3): 398 DOI: 10.1111/j.1467-7687.2012.01142.x

[xiii] Glass, B. D., Maddox, T. W., & Love, B.C. (2013). Real-Time Strategy Game Training: Emergence of a Cognitive Flexibility Trait. *PLoS ONE* 8(8)

[xiv] Granic, I., Lobel, A. & Engels, R. C. M. E. (2014). The Benefits of Playing Video Games. *American Psychologist*, 66-78

[xv] Granic, I., Lobel, A. & Engels, R. C. M. E. (2014). The Benefits of Playing Video Games. *American Psychologist*, 66-78

[xvi] Granic, I., Lobel, A. & Engels, R. C. M. E. (2014). The Benefits of Playing Video Games. *American Psychologist*, 66-78

[xvii] Altmann, M., Trafton, J.G. & Hambrick, D. Z. (2014) Momentary interruptions can derail the train of

thought. *Journal of Experimental Psychology: General,* Vol 143(1), 215-226.

[xviii] Cooper-Kahn, J., Dietzel, L. (2008) *Late, Lost, and Unprepared: A Parents' Guide to Helping Children with Executive Functioning,* Woodbine House, Bethesda, MD.

[xix] Christakis, D.A. et al (2004) 'Early television exposure and subsequent attentional problems in children', Pediatrics, 113 (4): 708–13

[xx] American Academy of Pediatrics, "Video Games Linked to Attention Problems in Children," press release, July 5, 2010, www.aap.org

[xxi] Dworak, M., Schierl, T., Bruns, T., & Strüder, H. K. (2007). Impact of singular excessive computer game and television exposure on sleep patterns and memory performance of school-aged children, *Pediatrics,* 120(5), 978-85 and Weaver, E., Gradisar, M., Dohnt, H., Lovato, N., Douglas, P. (2010). The effect of presleep video-game play on adolescent sleep. *Journal of Clinical Sleep Medicine,* 6(2), 184-89

[xxii] Kalnin, A. J., Wang, Y., Kronenberg, W. G., Mosier, K. M., Hummer, T. A., Dunn, D. W., Matthews, V. P. (2010). Short-term violent video game play by adolescents alters prefrontal activity during cognitive inhibition, *Media Psychology,* 13(2), 136-154

[xxiii] Christine Rosen, "The Myth of Multitasking, " *The New Atlantis,* Spring 2008, www.thenewatlantis.com

[xxiv] Fetler, M. (1984). Television viewing and school achievement. *Journal of Communication,* 34(2), 104-18.

[xxv] Calvert, S., & Wilson, B.J. (2008). Learning from Educational Media. In *The handbook of children, media, and development.* Chichester, U.K.: Wiley-Blackwell.

xxvi Gentile, D. A., Reimer, R., Nathanson, A. I., Walsh, D. A., Eisenmann, J. C. (2014). Protective effects of parental monitoring of children's media use: A prospective study. *JAMA Pediatrics*, 168(5), 479-84

xxvii Calvert, S. (2008). Attention and Learning from Media during Infancy and Early childhood. In *The handbook of children, media, and development*. Chichester, U.K.: Wiley-Blackwell. or Evans-Schmidt, M. Pempek, T.A., Kirkorian, H.L., Frankenfield, L.A., & Anderson, D.R. (?). The effects of background television on the toy play behavior of very young children. ..

xxviii Anderson, D.R., Evans-Schmidt, M., & Pempek, T.A. (2005) *TV and Toddlers*. Paper presented at the Society for Research on Child Development, Atlanta, GA.

xxix Brown, K. W. & Ryan, R. M. (2003). The benefits of being present: mindfulness and its role in psychological well-being, *Journal of Personality and Social Psychology*, 84(4):822-48.

xxx Thomée, S. (2012) ICT use and mental health in young adults. Effects of computer and mobile phone use on stress, sleep disturbances, and symptoms of depression. University of Gothenburg. Sahlgrenska Academy Retrieved from: http://hdl.handle.net/2077/28245

xxxi Park, Y., Fritz, C., Jex, S. M. (2011). Relationships between work-home segmentation and psychological detachment from work: the role of communication technology use at home. *Journal of Occupational Health Psychology*, 16(4):457-67.

xxxii Pocheptsova, Anastasiya (2012), "Cellphish Effects of Cell Phone Use," Rotman Magazine, 12(Fall), 111-113

xxxiii Shelton, J. T., Elliott, E. M., Eaves, S. T., Exner,

A. L. (2009). The distracting effects of a ringing cell phone: An inverstigation of the laboratory and the classroom setting, *Journal of Environmental Pscyhology*, (29)4, 513-21

[xxxiv] American Psychological Association (2006) Multitasking: Switching Costs. Retrieved from: http://www.apa.org/research/action/multitask.aspx

[xxxv] Sanbonmatsu, D. M., Strayer, D. L., Medeiros-Ward, N., & Watson, J. M. (2013). Who Multi-Tasks and Why? Multi-Tasking Ability, Perceived Multi-Tasking Ability, Impulsivity, and Sensation Seeking, PLoS ONE 8(1): e54402. doi:10.1371/journal.pone.0054402

[xxxvi] Calvert, S., & Wilson, B.J. (2008). Learning from Educational Media. In *The handbook of children, media, and development*. Chichester, U.K.: Wiley-Blackwell.

[xxxvii] Baranowski, T., Abdelsamad, D., Baranowski, J., O'Connor, T. M., Thompson, D., Barnett, A., … Chen, T.-A. (2012). Impact of an Active Video Game on Healthy Children's Physical Activity. *Pediatrics*, *129*(3), e636–e642. doi:10.1542/peds.2011-2050

[xxxviii] Khang, H., Kim, J.K. & Kim, Y. (2013) Self-traits and motivations as antecedents of digital media flow and addiction: The internet, mobile phones, and video games, *Computers in Human Behavior*, 29(6), 2416-2424

[xxxix] Bioulac, S., Arfi, L. & Bouvard, M.P. (2008) Attention deficit/hyperactivity disorder and video games: A comparative study of hyperactive and control children. *European Psychiatry*, 23(2), 134-141 and Weizman, A. & Weinstein, A.M. (2012) Emerging association between addictive faming and attention-deficit/hyperactivity disorder, *Current Psychiatry Reports*, 14(5), 590-597

[xl] Fung, D., Khoo, A., Li, D., Gentile, D.A., Choo, H., Sim, T. & Liau, A.K. (2011). Pathological video game use among youths: A two-year longitudinal study, *Pediatrics*, 127(2), 319-327

[xli] Yen, J.Y., Yen, C.F., Chen, C.S., Tang, T.C. & Ko, C.H. (2009) The association between adult ADHD symptoms and internet addiction among college students: The gender difference, *CyberPsychology & Behavior*, 12(2), 187-191

[xlii] Lorch, E.P., Milich, R. & Acevedo-Polakovich, I.D. (2007) Comparing television use and reading in children with ADHD and non-referred children across two age groups, *Media Psychology*, 9(2), 447-472

[xliii] Johnson, J.G., Cohen, P., Kasen, S. & Brook, J.S. (2007). Extensive television viewing and the development of attention and learning difficulties during adolescence, *Archives of Pediatrics & Adolescent Medicine*, 161(5), 480-486

[xliv] Rosen, C. (2008) "The Myth of Multitasking", *The New Atlantis*, Spring 2008, www.thenewatlantis.com

[xlv] Weiss, M.D., Baer, S., Allan, B.A., Saran, K. & Schibuk, H. (2011). The screens culture: impact on ADHD, *Attention Deficit Hyperactivity Disorder*, 3(4), 327-334

[xlvi] Tahiroglu, A.Y., Celik, G.G., Avci, A., Seydaoglu, G., Uzel, M. & Altunabas, H. (2010) Short-term effects of playing computer games on attention, *Journal of Attention Disorders*, 13(6), 668-676

[xlvii] Cardoso-Leite, P. & Bavelier, D. (2014). Video Game play, attention and learning: How to shape the development of attention and influence learning? *Current Opinion in Neurology*, 27(2), 185-191

[xlviii] Tahiroglu, A.Y., Celik, G.G., Avci, A., Seydaoglu,

G., Uzel, M. & Altunabas, H. (2010) Short-term effects of playing computer games on attention, *Journal of Attention Disorders*, 13(6), 668-676

[xlix] Li, X., Li, D. & Newman, J. (2013) Parental behavioral and psychological control and problematic internet use among Chinese adolescents: The mediating role of self-control, *Cyberpsychology, Behavior, and Social Networking*, 16(6), 442-447

[l] Lillard, A.S. & Peterson, J. (2011). The immediate impact of different types of television on young children's executive function, *Pediatrics*, 128(4), 644-949

[li] Mazurek, M.O. & Wenstrup, C. (2013). Television, video game and social media use among children with ASH and typically developing siblings, *Journal of Autism and Development Disorders*, 43(6) 1258-1271

[lii] Shane, H.C. & Albert, P.D. (2008). Electronic screen media for persons with autism spectrum disorders: Results of a survey, *Journal of Autism and Development Disorders*, 38(8), 1499-1508

[liii] Mazurek, M.O. & Wenstrup, C. (2013). Television, video game and social media use among children with ASH and typically developing siblings, *Journal of Autism and Development Disorders*, 43(6) 1258-1271

[liv] Engelhardt, C.R., Mazurek, M.O, & Sohl, K. (2013). Media Use and Sleep Among Boys with Autism Spectrum Disorder, ADHD, or Typical Development, *Pediatrics*, 1081-1089

[lv] Mazurek, Micah O., and Christopher R. Engelhardt. 2013. "Video Game Use and Problem Behaviors in Boys with Autism Spectrum Disorders." *Research in Autism Spectrum Disorders* 7(2):316–24.

[lvi] Gaylord-Ross, R.J., Haring, T.G., Breen, C. & Pitts-Conway, V. (1984). The training and generalization of social interaction skills with autistic youth. Journal of Applied Behaviour Analysis, 17, 229

[lvii] Griffiths, M. (2002) The educational benefits of videogames, *Education and Health*, 20(3), 47-51

[lviii] Lo, S-K., Wang, C-C. & Fang, W. (2005). Physical interpersonal relationships and social anxiety among online game players, *CyberPsychology & Behavior*, 8(1), 15-20

[lix] Lohaus, A., Ball, J., Klein-Hessling, J. & Wild, M. (2005). Relations between media use and self-reported symptomology in young adolescents, *Anxiety, Stress & Coping: An International Journal*, 18(4), 333-341

[lx] Shepherd, R. & Edelmann, R.J. (2005). Reasons for internet use and social anxiety, *Personality and Individual Differences*, 39(5), 949-958

[lxi] Marinelli, M., Sunyer, J., Alvarez-Pedrerol, M., Iniguez, C., Torrent, M., Vioque, J., ... Julvez, J. (2014). Hours of television viewing and sleep duration in children: A mulitcenter birth cohort study. *JAMA Pediatrics*, 168(5), 458-64

[lxii] Kouda, K., Fujoka, Y., Mase, T., Miyawaki, C, Okita, Y., Ishikawa, T. et al (2012). Combined influence of media use on subjective health in elementary school children in Japan: A population-based study, *BMC Public Health*, 12(432), 1-10

[lxiii] Helgason, A. R., Sigfusodottir, I. D., Kristjansson, A. L., & Fei, Y. (2013). Electronic Screen Use and Mental Wellbeing in 10-12-year-old-children. *European Journal of Public Health*, 23(3), 492-98

[lxiv] *Hart, A. (2013). The digital invasion: How technology is*

shaping you and your relationships. Grand Rapids, MI: Baker Books., 65.

[lxv] Yoon, J-S., Yang, S-J., Stewart, R., Lee, J-Y., Kim, J-M., Kim, S-W. et al. (2014). Prevalence and correlated of problematic internet experiences and computer-using time: A two-year longitudinal study in Korean school children, *Psychiatry Investigation*, 11(1), 24-31

[lxvi] Bryant, J., Carveth, R.A. & Brown, D. (1981). Television viewing and anxiety: An experimental examination, *Journal of Communication*, 31(1), 106-119

[lxvii] Szabo, A. & Hopkinson, K.L. (2007). Negative psychological effects of watching the news in the television: Relaxation or another intervention may be needed to buffer them, *International Journal of Behavioral Medicine*, 14(2), 57-62

[lxviii] Comer, J.S., Furr, J.M., Beidas, R.S., Babyar, H.M. & Kendall, P.C. (2008). Media use and children's perceptions of societal threat and personal vulnerability, *Journal of Clinical & Adolescent Psychology* 37(3), 622-630

[lxix] Szabo, A. & Hopkinson, K.L. (2007). Negative psychological effects of watching the news in the television: Relaxation or another intervention may be needed to buffer them, *International Journal of Behavioral Medicine*, 14(2), 57-62

[lxx] Ceyhan, A.A. & Ceyhan, E. (2008). Loneliness, depression, and computer self-efficacy as predictors of problematic internet use, *CyberPsychology & Behavior*, 11(6), 699-701

[lxxi] Harman, J.P., Hansen, C.E., Cochran, M.E., Lindsey, C.R. (2005). Liar, liar: Internet faking but not frequency of use affects social skills, self-esteem, social

anxiety and aggression, *CyberPsychology & Behavior*, 8(1), 1-6

[lxxii] Desjarlais, M. & Willoughby, T. (2010). A longitudinal study of the relation between adolescent boys and girls' computer use with friends and friendship quality: Support for the social compensation or the rich-get-richer hypothesis?, *Computers in Human Behavior*, 26(5), 896-905

[lxxiii] Selfhout, M.H.W., Branje, S.J.T., Delsing, M., ter Bogt, T.F.M. & Meeus, W.H.J. (2009) Different types of internet use, depression, and social anxiety: The role of perceived friendship quality, *Journal of Adolescence*, 32(4), 819-833

[lxxiv] Orue, I, Bushman, B.J., Calvete, E, Thomas, S., Orobio de Castro, B. & Hutteman, R. (2011). Moneky see, monkey do, monkey hurt: Longitudinal effects of exposure to violence on children's aggressive behavior, *Social Psychological and Personality Science*, 2(4), 432-437

[lxxv] Anderson, C. A., Carnagey, N. L., Fanagan, M., Benjamin Jr., A. J., Eubanks, J., & Valentine, J. C. (2004) Violent video games: Specific effects of violent content of aggressive thought and behavior, *Advances in Experimental Social Psychology*, 36, 199-249

[lxxvi] Beresin, E.V. (2014) The Impact of Media Violence on Children & Adolescents: Opportunities for Clinical Intervention, *American Academy of Child & Adolescent Psychiatry*, retrieved from: www.aacap.org

[lxxvii] Verlinden, M., Tiemeier, H., Veenstra, R., Mieloo, C.L., Jansen, W., Jaddoe, V.W.V et al (2014). Television viewing through ages 2-5 years and bullying involvement in early elementary school, *BMC Public Health*, 14(1), 157

[lxxviii] Tandon, P.S., Zhou, C., Lozano, P. & Christakis,

D.A. (2011). Preschoolers' total daily screen time at home and by type of child care, *The Journal of Pediatrics*, 158)2), 297-300

lxxix Mendelsohn, A.L., Berkule, S.B., Tomopoulos, S., Tamis-LeMonda, C.S., Huberman, H.S., Alvir, J. et al (2008). Infant television and video exposure associated with limited parent-child verbal interactions in low socioeconomic status households, *Archives of Pediatrics & Adolescent Medicine*, 162(5), 411-417

lxxx Wen, L.M., Rissel, C. & Xu, H. (2014). Associations of maternal influences with outdoor play and screen time of two-year olds: Findings from the Healthy Beginnings Trial, *Journal of Pediatrics and Child Health*, 1-7

lxxxi Timperio, A, Salmon, J., Ball, K., te Velde, S.J. Brug, J. & Crawford, D. (2012). Neighborhood characteristics and TV viewing in youth: Nothing to do but watch TV?, *Journal of Science and Medicine in Sport*, 15(2), 122-128

lxxxii Linebarger, D.L. & Piotrowski, J.T. (2009). TV as storyteller: How exposure to television narratives impacts at-risk preschoolers' story knowledge and narrative skills, *British Journal of Developmental Psychology*, 27(1), 47-69

lxxxiii Wilson, B.J. (2011) *Media Violence and Aggression in Youth* In The Handbook of Children, Media and Development edited by Calvert, S.J. & Wilson, B.J.

Stay Informed -

Family TechKnowledge
Helping Families Understand the Impact of Modern
Media & Entertainment
www.michelleaellisor.com/FTK/

About the Author

Michelle Ellisor, LMFT, is a Licensed Marriage and Family Therapist with a passion for helping parents and families find a healthy way to function in an often frenzied modern world. In addition to her background in counseling and mental health, she has a bachelor's degree in film production, which highlights her early interest in media and technology. She has given presentations on a number of parenting, technology and social media topics. She is also the creator of the *Family TechKnowledge* campaign, which shares information for families about the impact of modern media and entertainment.